MY FRIEND STEWART

BY

ANTHONY DAY

Published by Columbine Pictures Press
Copyright © 2018 Anthony Day and Columbine Pictures Press

ISBN: 0995555699
ISBN-13: 9780995555693

For Stewart
best friends forever

1

It all started for me, thirteen years ago, in Canterbury. I was volunteering at the YMCA Training Centre, Clarkson House, helping the long-term unemployed write their letters, CVs, applications forms and undertake job searches on the internet, in exchange for using their facilities to do my own research. It was a great system and helped me out a lot as I started my business.

With me not being 'real' staff, the clients didn't feel they were under pressure when with me and were not being judged or forced into putting something down, as if they were a statistic to be stamped, indexed, filed and forgotten, but could have a laugh and a joke as they struggled with their application forms and CVs and so were grateful for my help.

I know of several during my time there who got decent jobs as a result and, until they changed location to Margate, YMCA Training was a place that encouraged success. Run by Mark Cable and Richard, they helped give those clients a work-orientated mindset. Located in a 1960s office block just outside the city's walls, looking out towards the Dane John, it had the feeling of a business and anyone seeing you enter would have thought you worked for a company in one of the offices, so it was pretty well the best place to be.

But when it moved to Margate, to an old classroom block away from the main body of a now defunct school, which itself felt like an afterthought, tucked out of the way down some dingy back street, with nothing around but boarded-up shops, flats and a potholed road, a lifeless, two-storey square blot on the landscape, it was less inspiring, if not a bit depressing for anyone with an aspiration to move on with their life.

But I had my business up and running by then and wasn't part of that move. Everything that happened leading to this story happened there in Canterbury.

One day, I don't recall when, Stewart came to Clarkson House, sent by the Jobcentre to spend six weeks looking for work. He was overweight, shy, inarticulate, couldn't use a computer and spoke in a blunt, monosyllabic way, which made people think he was either stupid or rude. When the others would group around by the newspapers, with their disposable cups of tea or coffee, whining on about being unemployed, the football, the soaps and the reality TV shows or the events in the national papers exposing the lack of morals of some female pop star who was no longer tabloid flavour of the month and annoyed they couldn't smoke inside, he would be in the corner, not saying anything, looking lost, watching the clock and waiting to go home.

Very few people it seemed wanted to give him the time of day.

Now I'm no saint, probably having more in common with the Leslie Charteris character than Saint Jude, but occasionally I'd stop, look at a paper and say a few words, nothing about anything much and he'd reply with a 'Yeah' and that was that.

I helped with his CV. He'd been a labourer in London, had worked on making kitchen units until the firm had moved away and he had undertaken some voluntary work at the gardens at Strode Park and the kitchens at Whitstable's Umbrella Centre, where he now lived.

He was taking medication for depression and other medication, for what at the time I didn't know and wasn't bothered about, but he told me this and I had noticed that he had self-harmed in the past. You couldn't help but notice the faint scars on his lower arm.

Soon enough, his six weeks were up and he went. Within that year, I too was off, America for a while, then a bit of nomadic life for a few months until I eventually found a place to put down some roots.

It was now 2005.

I was living in Seasalter, a district on the outskirts of Whitstable.

And it was here that our adventure began.

2

I'd been shown around and decided to take the flat because of the view.

Stunning it was, over the marshes. Most the houses and other flats facing that way only had a view of the bushes or sat overlooking one of the two static-home parks, whereas I had the clear gap with Graveney and Monk's Hill in the distance, the sea and the Isle of Sheppey Nature Reserve to my right, and not enough of the old Thanet Way or the railway line to spoil any of it.

I had two great shops, one close to hand, which didn't sell so much fresh produce but was great for tins, milk and frozen stuff, and, ten minutes' gentle walk away, a Spar, which would later become a Londis then a Co-op, always good for a choice of items and fresh fruit and veg.

As it was February and cold, for the first couple of weeks, it was paint the walls, get some furniture and basically make it habitable. After a few days I ventured out and tried the two shops and a couple of weeks later, on one sunny day in late March or early April, needing some milk, I went out for a walk and decided to go through the estate for the first time to try and find the short route to the Spar rather than just following the main road round all the time.

I had been to the Spar twice before by now and curiosity told me that the road that ran beside the shop towards the estate, even if it was only linked by an alleyway, must link up with the rest of the estate at some point and I was determined to find out just where.

In fact, it was much easier than I thought and I was annoyed with myself for not finding it sooner. But it was also the day that would change everything about my life, my outlook, my priorities, everything.

I would change from being a person who kept himself private and got on with his own things whilst being around more boastful or more conceited people who liked to go on about how wonderful or how successful their little lives were, when, in truth, they weren't any more successful or wonderful than all those people whose CVs I'd helped fill in. Only, unlike them, they still had a job and an income, which actually meant really they could afford a better pair of jeans and a takeaway to impress me with. However, even if they had aspirations, they never followed them up, so really in their company I was little more than a passive spectator. Instead, over the next eight years, I became a person who wanted to make a change, wanting always the best for someone else, not just myself, a person who cared for and cared about someone other than me and became compassionate, tired of vain, silly people, to the point where I couldn't be bothered about them anymore, eventually cutting them all out of my life completely.

Now I wouldn't say I hadn't had friends in the past. They come and go as life gets in the way and most of them just fade away. You don't realise they've gone until you either accidently bump into them again and realise you've both changed so much you just know you're not going to bump into each other ever again or realise you're not doing something anymore, like being in a writers' club, which you used to do and was really the only place you saw them. So, as with most friends, it's the shared interest you both have which draws you together and when either one of you can't do that anymore, the friendship drifts apart.

We can all count hundreds of friends that have passed through our lives but it's very rare for any of us to find one or two true friends, that shared soul, that person you just like, because....?

So as I was making my way down the road, like a fish out of water, not really sure what I was doing but basically looking at everything to familiarise myself with it for future reference, and passed a few flats and the bus stop, I noticed this guy sitting on the brick retaining wall that was like a ha-ha wall, partly submerged in the grass verge between pavement and road, that all the properties in the centre of the estate have round their bin porches. He was just sitting there in the sun looking as bored as anything, as if he was waiting for someone but they hadn't shown up. He looked up at me just as I was passing and instinctively, because I'm a friendly kind of guy, I said 'Hi' with a great big cheesy grin on my face and he seemed surprised. His head rocked back as if he couldn't believe I'd noticed him, let alone said anything, and after a moment he said 'Hi' back.

I carried on to the shop and on my way back he was still sitting there, just as before, and as I passed, this time on the other side of the road, I waved to him. He saw me and just nodded.

I could tell there was something familiar about him and I don't mean because I'd seen him twenty minutes before. Whilst I was having my cup of tea I realised that, before I shot off to the States, he was the guy I'd seen at Tower Parade sitting on a bench each morning when I'd been going to catch the bus to Canterbury and I used to say 'hi' to him then too, although I'd always been in a hurry and hadn't taken much notice, however I still had a nagging feeling I'd seen him somewhere else, but just couldn't place where.

It felt weird that a person I'd known on nodding terms when living on the other side of town should now be living on the same estate I'd just moved on to over a year later. At least, I reasoned, as a nodding acquaintance he would be able to tell me which of the three nearby pubs was worth visiting as now the flat was painted and the mismatched furniture was laid out in a homely if somewhat random tribute to interior design, I felt it was time to go meet people.

So, I decided, from then on, I'd pay all my bills at the Spar and I would go that way at least once a week on the off-chance that I might see him again, as saying 'Hi' to someone makes you feel you belong there, especially when you don't know anyone yet, so at least I would still feel connected to the human race.

For a few weeks it was all a bit hit-and-miss but one day I was heading back and I didn't have any work planned for a couple of weeks plus it was a warm, sunny day so I stopped to talk to him. We did that very British thing and just talked about the weather and the buses but it became something we regularly did as I would now see him every trip and so, a couple of months or so later, I asked if he wanted to come round for a cup of tea.

We went to my flat and it was then that he asked me if I had been at Clarkson House. At that moment I remembered he was the quiet fellow, the one no one talked to and who suffered from depression, who I'd know during my time at the YMCA. In my defence I'd met a lot of people there, so many names and faces, but he'd remembered and now it made sense as to why he'd waved to me all those times when he was living at Tower Parade. I didn't let on, but I did feel a bit embarrassed about not realising where we'd first met for a while.

He noticed that I didn't have any television. I had a set, but no aerial. In fact, there was no evidence that there had ever been an aerial in the flat. A neighbour two down from me used a portable and I suspected the people before me did as well but, on the whole, I'd grown tired of TV at that time, hadn't seen any for a long time, so I wasn't in a hurry to get an aerial of any kind.

I wasn't a fan of the soaps, or reality shows, DIY or consumer programmes so hadn't missed it, all which he found a bit curious and so, on the spur of the moment, he asked if I'd like to come round to his on Saturday evening to watch the football on 'Match of the Day'.

I said, 'I'll come round after dinner. I'll bring a movie and we can make a night of it.'

After all, it seemed a bit mean to just go round for half ten, watch the games and then head back home. To me, that felt a bit like I would be taking advantage of his generosity, so the least I could do was bring something round and make a night of it.

He said, 'Okay.'

From that moment on we saw each other at first once a week, for a cup of tea at mine, then going round to his to watch usually a movie but occasionally some show on the TV, before the football every Saturday.

After a few weeks, he came round one Saturday to find me hanging out the washing.

'What you doing?'

'Hanging out the washing.'

'But you ain't got a washing machine.'

'I know. I do it by hand.'

I made the tea and, as we sat on the sofas and listened to the live football match while my dinner cooked, I could see him thinking about something, and not the football as he didn't react when they scored, and at first I thought it was something he was concerned about.

So I asked, 'What is it?'

'You can use my washing machine if you like.'

'Thanks.' I was genuinely surprised and thought it a generous offer. I knew I had enough clothes to do a large wash once every couple of weeks but then I had a thought. A full load takes over an hour and was a Saturday night really the time to do it? The noise of the machine for one thing would ruin the movie so then I added, 'I could do it on a Sunday if that's alright?'

'Do it when you like.'

'No, Sunday would be ideal. I could cook us a proper Sunday dinner if you like, whilst it's washing. Been a while since I've had a real proper Sunday dinner.'

'Okay.'

From then on we shared the cost of a proper home-cooked Sunday lunch and for the first time since I'd left home, I was cooking a proper family meal.

So slowly, as the summer progressed, we started to see each other more frequently. We had our Saturdays as they'd always been. He would come round for tea and to listen to the football whilst I had my dinner. After that, we'd go round to his, get the full results on Final Score, then either play some computer games first or, if there was a game show or something like that, watch that first, then the computer games during the Lotto and the grim drama before switching back to the TV for the football or, if we didn't fancy a game, we'd watch a movie instead.

Then, as we got more into the computer games, I'd come round a couple of times a week until, by 2008, I'd be seeing him every day, a couple of hours each weekday evening, and most Saturdays for about seven hours and the same on Sundays.

3

In fact, by 2008, of all my friends, he was the one I was spending the most time with. I even found myself when with a film-geek friend of mine in Herne Bay, who I would see once every couple of months for a Saturday afternoon of cheesy old films, keeping an eye on the time, planning to head back so not to miss Final Score.

Also on those Saturdays, instead of cooking at home, I'd have a light meal with Stewart and, although I had a lot of work to keep me busy, life seemed to be drawing us ever closer.

So why spend so much time together?

After all, I had planned to join a Whitstable amateur dramatics group, a writers' group and go occasionally to Herne Bay to watch a movie, though there was a pub cinema in town and I saw one film there before it closed. I was thinking of doing so much when I first moved on to the estate. It's what my life had been like in Canterbury, Herne, etc, etc, so joining and doing those things seemed just natural.

However, I suppose those things are all about meeting up with people who think the same as you, to talk about the same old things. It's like being in a room of nodding dogs. No one really has a dissimilar view. But watching a film, say, that you love, finding someone who knows nothing about it and then hoping they're going to like it, and they do, bringing someone new into your own world, is more fun, more interesting than having to get all dressed up, have a shave and having to be happy and enthused all the time around people that, in truth, you hardly know but for a shared interest, which seems only to be held together by the promise of alcohol afterwards.

It's probably why, when it works, families don't go out much and the weekend pub scene is really the preserve of the old singles and the young, who are usually single looking to mingle. Everyone who's watching something like 'I'm a Celebrity' or whatever are usually comfortable with each other and enjoying a shared experience without the need for a hangover in the morning to say they've had a good time.

In a way we were the perfect couple. I'm imaginative and creative and so stopped us getting into a TV rut as it were. That's why we never needed the soaps or the 'Celebs' shows. He was more practical and actually a very sensitive soul. Over the course of the first year or so he came to realise I didn't care about how he dressed, if he'd had a shave or a haircut or if he'd worn a T-shirt for a month, and it didn't matter what he said.

I was there as a friend and he appreciated it.

So what was he like?

Well, to know that, first you have to know about why he was how he was and why people who are basically judgemental about everything and know next to nothing about anything never saw the man inside and lost that opportunity to enrich their own lives.

Physically, at the beginning he was large, with a double chin, probably about 48 inches around the stomach and only five feet five tall, but thirteen years later he was a lot slimmer, no double chin, at his heaviest, after Christmas, 45 inches at the waist but averaging during those last four years 43 inches but still five feet five tall.

Though overweight, he was still charming. He had a kindly, warm face, long but round, sort of cherublike, a bit like John Candy in his early days or Larry Miller when he still had hair, but with the smile of the Stay Puff Marshmallow Man from 'Ghostbusters', with brown eyes that looked at you with an innocence you often only see in children.

He was clean-shaven, had some old tattoos on his arms, was left-handed and often wore his watch on his left wrist and a copper bracelet on his right. He liked to dress in jogging bottoms or jeans, sweatshirts and T-shirts and wore trainers but then so does nearly every single person living in Whitstable if not East Kent or the UK at large.

But that's not what a person is. That's the culture or the image they want to project based purely on their income. Had he had the money, he could have had a Savile Row suit, ostrich-leather shoes and a Rolex.

What he was, was the person inside all that. A softly spoken, gentle man, who wanted to be liked but was always mindful of how he looked and often took things too much to heart, wanted to make people happy, generous to a fault, loyal, actually very intelligent but lacking the belief in himself to use his intelligence at first, trustworthy, witty, shy, awkward at times, lacking in confidence and suffering from mental illness.

He was suffering from schizophrenia.

The signs are different for everyone, which is why it can take a while to diagnose and is why only a GP who's known you for years is qualified to assess your condition and, for the thirteen years I knew him, why he would continuously go through cycles of relapse and remission. To my shame, for the first couple of years, I had stupidly thought the remissions meant he was getting better and would get angry at the relapses, not at him but angry thinking either the doctors or something I'd done had made things worse and only with time did I come to understand things better.

But, by the time of the crash in 2008 and all the things that happened to me in general then, I realised how fragile everything about a person really is. We can all, say, get depressed for a while, or anxious, but normally we have the tools inside us to overcome these feelings. Schizophrenia robs a person of this and there is no drug or operation that can restore it so I learnt to ride out the relapses and pull him through to the remissions, which, as time progressed, became more frequent and longer lasting.

Schizophrenia is a serious disorder which affects how a person thinks, feels and acts. Someone with schizophrenia may have difficulty distinguishing between what is real and what is imaginary. Hallucinations, these he had, his demons, as he often heard sounds and told me he heard voices and couldn't distinguish at times between those in his head and those of his neighbours being just a little too noisy.

They may be unresponsive or withdrawn, which he often was in the early years, and may have difficulty expressing normal emotions in social situations, which he struggled with all the time.

Contrary to public perception, schizophrenia is not split or multiple personalities. The vast majority of people with schizophrenia are not violent and do not pose a danger to others. Schizophrenia is not caused by childhood experiences, poor parenting or lack of willpower.

When I first met him on the estate, he suffered a lot from voices that weren't there, was paranoid people were always talking about him or watching him in a critical way, which made it difficult to be anywhere with large crowds, shopping for instance, or to go somewhere new, so joining a drama club was out of the question.

It also meant if some drunken idiots were having a slanging match near to his flat, he would worry that it was either about him or would spill into his flat somehow. If I was there, he didn't worry so much as I didn't worry but I would often see the panic on his face until I'd made some glib remark and put him at ease.

I gave him my mobile number and that helped too as he could call me up when he had a problem and I could either give him some advice or sort it out by coming over a bit earlier and, on the occasions that some idiots did kick off, I was there to reassure him and things were fine.

His illness manifested itself in other ways too as, when he got frustrated or excited about something, he'd end up speaking in a peculiar or nonsensical way but asking him to say it again often helped him to rein it in and become clearer. I think that's probably why most of the time he liked short sentences, as he felt people wouldn't judge him as stupid if he didn't have to have a conversation with them.

He could be indifferent to very important situations but, as time went by, you could see he did feel and was affected by everything around him. He just didn't know how to show it because, I suspect, he didn't want to be judged as being soft or harsh or whatever so he, for the most part, showed nothing but as I became indifferent to his indifference, he began to start opening up a bit more. He'd make a comment about something and, not being put down for it, he would open up and talk more about things and would, except for when he was in relapse, when there was just the two of us, we could talk about and discuss something we'd just watched.

His writing was like a young child's and he had trouble remembering which way round the letters went. He had trouble working out sums and no amount of explaining how to take a long sum, add it up in little groups, then add the groups together worked completely as he would often write the sum out several times and if he made one mistake, and the numbers didn't match up after three of four goes, he'd panic. I'd do it and confirm that usually he'd got it right first time and if he tried to do like I would, work the sum out in his head, he would start playing the air piano. He'd look at his hands and you'd see the fingers move as he counted, which looked as if he was playing an invisible keyboard, but he could never be sure the sum was right and would then, after a good half an hour or so, ask me what the answer was anyway.

Yet for all of that, he was often right. His grasp on things may have deteriorated from when he was younger but not his intelligence.

He had worked on building sites and in constructing kitchens before so measuring and using maths a lot and reading instructions had been his life. But now, also lacking confidence, at times he generally struggled. Shopping together, I could keep a general tally as we went round and knew within £10 what the final cost would be but he couldn't. He had to go by how much room was left in the trolley and hope for the best. However, between us, somehow, both systems worked.

He could go from being really bubbly, almost hyperactive, chirpy and full of life one day to the next day being so depressed that he couldn't get out of bed and disinterested in the world. In our early years, he was full of morbid desires, often trying to get a reaction out of me by talking about wanting to kill himself, though being a bit of a Goth myself, someone talking about morbid things like death and existence doesn't shock me. I'm quite happy to chat about those things really.

I would often say to him, to get him out of these moods, 'I wouldn't kill yourself if I was you. After all, no one knows if what they say in the Bible is true and it could be just like Beetlejuice for all you know.'

He'd give me a wry smile and that was the end of that. I think the idea of spending two hundred years waiting to fill in more forms was enough to keep anyone alive.

His person hygiene never suffered. However, the flat was always untidy and could have done with a clean. It never smelt bad or got so awful it was unbearable but it seemed to be forever in a managed state of chaos, as if 'Dave Lister' had been a roommate and had just stepped out to get a curry. But it wasn't something worth getting on his back about.

He could be irrational, irritable, angry or fearful about minor things but, as time went by, less so as he became reassured knowing I was there to support him when things got out of control.

Yet he kept pets, which always thrived. One in particular, Jason the cat, had been the runt of a litter nobody wanted so Stewart took him. Jason might have ended up a house cat but he was a healthy lively animal, who was spoilt rotten.

So at first we must have seemed more like the Odd Couple from Neil Simon's play, though the traits of each character were shared out between us. I suppose the reason our friendship worked was similar to the way the real friendship between Laurel and Hardy was so strong as, despite our differences, we both clicked and felt so comfortable in each other's company that, after a while, after a slow start, it became somewhat difficult to be apart.

4

For those first three years, we seemed to play a lot of computer games. It suited me as I spent a lot of time travelling to France, Germany and Holland for the odd two weeks or weekends away for work, so spending the time with someone just doing something simple for the rest of the time was just what I needed as much as he needed my companionship.

We had three games in particular that appealed to us and which we played together. He preferred to play platform games alone. Football, car racing on set race tracks and street racing, where the concept is a race down streets, dodging cars, and street furniture and so on, a bit like the Gumball Rally, were what we played.

Football we played the most, in that it was the one we always played together at the same time. The car games we'd take in turns. He didn't like the split screen because it would confuse him as to which side was which, so one of us would go first the then other, but the problem with the car games was that we both had totally different play set-up styles. I preferred the driver's view so you only had the clocks on screen, even though it's not like driving for real as you don't have any view of the car. I found that easier than having the whole car on screen, which was Stewart's style. As we got to know the circuits and play those games more, I became better at the circuits more quickly and once he felt he was too far behind, he would stop taking his go and would instead just watch me play.

Even when he'd suggest we'd should play one of the car games, he'd be there, lying on the sofa, watching for an hour or so as I'd wrestle with the circuit and so, after a while, once I'd reached the level my skills or lack of them deserved, I too would lose interest and without someone else playing it with the same visual set up, to bounce ideas off each other how to get to the next level or how to improve, the games would get abandoned and gather dust until we'd next visit the Game Store in Canterbury.

Football on the other hand was a different experience. Difficult each time at first but as we got used to the games, it became much easier and more predictable to play. However, just as it was beginning to get boring, the next version would come out and so it all started all over again.

I could tell he was enthusiastic about the football as, for the first month or so, we'd play four games every night I was round, probably having more draws than either of us winning, but once each of us had found the teams we played well with, after a few months, we had high-scoring games and largely repeat wins for whoever played and won that particular combination last time round. Because Stewart didn't want anyone else to come over and join in, as we got to know each other's play too well, the fun of the game diminished and we'd end up watching a bit more television until the next version arrived, setting the whole cycle going again.

So what was his flat like?

It was laid out well for playing games and watching movies, in that originally there was a sofa against the long wall up by the window and a corner unit, which was where Stewart sat, with the most commanding view of the TV. On a longer corner unit was the widescreen TV. There were two armchairs, one at right angles to the other and in line with the bottom of the coffee table, on which he had his fruit bowls, remotes and so on. Sitting on that chair, I could see the TV and Stewart, handy when playing computer games.

That chair also had a footstall which I used when we were just watching the telly. We would also chat, though for the most part at that time, I did most of the talking.

But by 2008 Stewart had bought a double sofa suite with a single armchair, though the layout stayed the same. From then on, he had two sofas against the long wall.

This was the first time he'd spent more than a couple of years in any given place, so at last he was setting down roots and, as he was confident with me, knowing I didn't care what he liked or how he wanted to decorate his place, that was up to him.

At first he'd spent a lot of time printing off and framing pictures of actresses he admired as well as dragons, landscapes and cats but all these pictures apart from two disappeared as a combination of more shelving going up and the purchase of better pictures, such as a Broch and a Salvador Dali print, three seaside boats from the Whitstable gift shops and other things like that took their place.

The flat had a cosy atmosphere with a nice use of space as well but an accident with the kitten Jason knocking over the TV led to us putting the replacement up on the wall and, from then on, I had to sit on the second sofa and the armchair became the depository, ending up with such a mountain on it that it became a bit like climbing K2 to switch the corner lamp on and off.

Because of the awkward way he used to sit or lie on the sofa, a surfeit of cushions made life comfortable for him but for me so many cushions didn't and no sooner did I get rid of one than he'd buy a replacement so there was yet another to remove and that's why in the end, half the cushions from the sofa ended up on that armchair.

5

Space, however, and its use, was always an issue and a serious part of his condition.

He suffered from agoraphobia, part of his anxiety disorder characterized by symptoms of fear in situations where he perceived the environment to be unsafe with no easy way to escape. These situations can include open spaces, public transport, shopping centres or simply being outside the home, which is why he struggled at times to go into town or to try anything new and he needed to be home by early evening.

The first time I had encountered this was on a trip to Tesco and I had thought at first, because he was overweight, that his heavy breathing was down to being out of breath, making, like so many ignorant people do, the wrong assumption, until I noticed as we had a cup of tea in the cafe afterwards, before going back for the bus, that he was shaking. Then the penny dropped and then I realized that the larger crowds as it got near to Christmas were the reason for his anxiety attack.

In fact it became a good clue to when he was suffering an anxiety attack. I now understood when he was at the edge, almost unable to cope, and now knowing the signs, when these things happened again over the years, instead of dismissing them as most of us would do and think 'go on a diet and you wouldn't be so tired', believing that was why he was puffing a bit, I could calm him down with a reassuring smile, a hand to the arm, a joke or change of subject and suddenly the heavy breathing and the panicked look would disappear. Despite his appearance, I quickly discovered he would end up no more out of breath and panting than any of us would normally do. He wouldn't be any more breathless just going up some stairs or walking to the shop than I would be if I was taking a brisk walk. He might have been overweight but he wasn't unfit.

It was the anxiety that gave him the appearance of being unfit. When he was in remission, he always going out to town, spending an hour walking around the shops and sometimes when really restless he would go for long walks to the beach and back. It was only when he was in relapse that he couldn't get out of bed, so it was really no surprise he could walk three miles briskly and feel no worse than I would and yet so easy to misread until you knew.

There were other obvious signs too that were obvious once I understood them. His need to buy things he didn't need, objects for objects' sake, unless he was filling all the spaces in his home, to build a wall around him, to keep the unseen terrors that haunted him outside, building with these objects a fortress to protect himself.

I wonder if he was still suffering with the hallucinations or fears that if there was a space, something might get there when he was sleeping, as over the years, I did try to help him de-clutter to make life easier for himself, only for it to work for a few weeks before a new set of clutter replaced it all.

It was also that, despite keeping himself clean and tidy, washing his clothes and so on regularly as we all do, his house cleaning was less vigorous. Yes, he would do it, like vacuum the carpets, but only in the areas where we walked or around the bird cages when they were emptied, so dusting shelves, getting those webs out of the far corner of the room behind the TV for example, no, they weren't a priority. Nothing that meant moving out the DVD piles or any other fortification was worth the trouble to clean behind.

The lounge was one thing, as in a strange way, the clutter in the end, didn't really get in our way. The room's layout meant, apart from a couple of lamps and putting a DVD on, there wasn't anything to get in our way, though when the cat Jason arrived, cat toys became more like landmines between the coffee table and TV but, for that, you'd have to blame the cat.

But the other rooms the clutter did cause a certain amount of problem.

The bedroom was inaccessible. When he brought the cruiser bike, it wouldn't fit in the box room, so it had to go in the bedroom. As it would only slot in between the bed and chest of drawers, to get to the tumble dryer, it meant you had to climb over the corner of the bed to get past the handlebars. Not a big problem and nothing you could really blame him for, but there would have been more space in the bedroom had it not been for the mound of clean clothes on an old armchair, that again was like another fortification against the outside world, which basically reduced the bedroom space to a narrow strip between the door and the window. Once the bike filled that space, it meant there was no option other than to climb over the bed to get to the window end of the room.

The bathroom became almost a shrine to the bubble bath and shampoo bottle. Now he was a very clean person, having a bath every day, so having more than one shampoo or bubble-bath bottle wasn't a surprise, especially as we both often bought the products when on offer, such as buy one get one free, knowing that at some point we'd use them, but it was the space again.

He got obsessed with first filling the space behind the taps before putting bottles all along the complete edge of the bath, the same way as some people put 'tea lights' around the edge to relax. Then the windowsill and every shelf were filled to overflowing with cleaning, shaving and dental products.

Again, not too much of a problem but it was the kitchen which, especially in the later years, did start to feel all boxed in.

What made it worse was that as soon as I helped him find a solution, such as a plate stacker to reduce the space the plates took up so glasses and bowls could go into the cupboards to free up some of the worktop, he'd then buy a jar or second breadbin and fill the space up again.

Even if we moved everything to make it more efficient and threw away the old chipped crockery he didn't use, making space for a microwave, the blender and filter coffee machine and leaving a little bit of room in front to still open a tin or place a pot when working on a meal, within a fortnight something new would be in that space.

Before the austerity cuts, he had carers, who would come and see him once a week, and though they meant well, trying to get him to clear up the draining board or get rid of clutter didn't work.

I found that a lateral approach, like calling the groaning and overloaded draining board a kerplunk and reminding him that replacing plates would be an expensive hobby, worked when it got too overloaded and he broke a lot less from them on.

We brought a pot stand for the saucepans, to clear the top of the cooker, only for him to then buy a poacher, a fish pan, a pasta pot and another saucepan and fill the space up again.

Okay, those items were useful. We used them several times, just as we used the normal pots and pans, but a lot of the jars and biscuit barrels that filled the space weren't. It was just as if he had an overwhelming need to fill the space. By 2014, and despite a third clear-out by 2015, there was never a free bit of space in that kitchen, even drink bottles ending up on the floor like a bastion around the chest freezer.

I had at first thought the hoarding and clutter was just that but, over the years, as I observed the bad times, I realised that clutter, like having three radios in the lounge, wasn't just clutter, it was a defence, either to keep things out or, as in the case of the radios, a backup to stay in touch with the world. If one should break down, there was a spare. I found that the moment I stopped seeing it as clutter and recognised it as a symptom of his condition, I became relaxed, which in turn relaxed him and, apart from the occasional purge, usually instigated at his own request as the good times returned, we left the clutter where it was.

6

Sometime around 2010 he had passed out in the street whilst out for a walk in Whitstable. Paramedics were called and he'd been brought home but no one knew why he had come over all dizzy and nothing more was said.

Then one night as I was watching TV, I heard a crash. He had fallen in the bathroom and I found him on the floor shaking and unconscious. At first, I thought he'd struck his head, tripped on a bath mat or something, but I couldn't see any blood and he was still breathing. With a few gentle words and a little gentle shake from me, as if waking someone who was asleep, he revived. I called an ambulance and got him a sweet tea while we waited. They checked him out, gave him the all-clear and went.

Twice more this happened.

Each time they took him to Canterbury Hospital and, after waiting for over two hours in A&E, we'd head back home, wondering what was going on. I knew he drank a lot of cola, three litres a day on average, sometimes a little less, in a mixture of those large plastic bottles and cans. The only time he drank less cola was the Sunday dinner that I was cooking, which might have been getting slightly bigger as the time had moved on, the amount of vegetables with it increasing as I'd become more and more adventurous, using the various versions from the various cookbooks I had at the time.

On the weekdays, he was still doing his own thing. He was eating or rather preparing meals that weren't very healthy and they made the Sunday dinner look like a vegan's salad.

Because he had no real interest in food and wasn't confident in his abilities, everything was simple and basic. Either from his past or as part of his condition, he had a fear he might starve the next day so his own portions he prepared were often large. Frequently it was a fine balancing job to bring the plate through to the lounge without spilling the food, though it was just as likely half of it would end up in the bin as he would never eat it all.

Actually, he refuted the popular myth, if you eat less and move more, you stay thin. He didn't eat much and before the first collapse was very active, often walking to town, going out most days even in the rain and, though he cooked more, he ate less than I did. I may have cycled everywhere but working from home I went out less than he did, only when I had to, so really he should have been slimmer than me if that mantra was actually true.

It wasn't so much the volume of food he was eating but the content. Sugar, especially in drinks, seems harmless at first because you can't see that you're piling on the calories. It's obvious a large burger's full of calories but a glass of coke, surely that's just full of bubbles. He only really drank less of it on the Sunday when he'd had a really filling meal.

His weight gain over the years before we met up on the estate was more likely because of the cola and snacking between mealtimes, when the cola didn't make him feel full, as he'd often miss out on breakfast and a midday lunch, only actually having an evening meal.

But a typical meal at the time was big on starches and protein and hardly anything else.

He'd often have something like seven boiled spuds, a spoonful of peas and either a couple of burgers, fish fingers, pie, bacon or sausages. On the face of it, nothing wrong, other than the huge amount of potatoes, but the quality of the burgers, pies and sausages in particular was horrendous.

Like the occasional ready meal he'd buy. They were the cheapest, nastiest things available in the local shops, such as the store's own so-called value brand, which were half the price of their market leader or less. If you take the burgers alone, not just half the price, but where you get something like four to six in the expensive brand and something like sixteen to twenty-four of the cheap brand and you have agoraphobia issues, for half the price you can buy between eight or twelve dinners and a large bag of his other nemesis at the time, chips, then it was no surprise his freezer was full of that sort of junk.

So the burgers shrinking by half as some of the fat poured out didn't matter to him. He couldn't cope with shopping and, as long as he had his comfort supply of sweets, of which he would pop a half dozen or so during a TV show, the fewer shopping trips he had to make the better as far he was concerned.

His other habit at the time was opening a packet of biscuits and saying, 'I'm just having a couple.'

Then take two handfuls, about eight in total.

Sweets were the same. He'd open a family-size bag of Skittles, intending to have just a handful and within an hour the bag would be gone.

When the deep depression would take hold, for days, if not weeks, I'd come round after dinner and find him still lying in bed, having not got up for the day and not really able to function properly even by the time I'd go home. He wasn't getting much exercise either then.

His doctor did some tests and it turned out he had type 2 diabetes. This meant our cosy Sunday dinners had to change.

As my skills had improved, so had our menus and Sunday dinner had become a three-course affair with a bottle of wine. It was all either of us had to eat on that day but not ideal if you have diabetes.

So Sunday dinner became a bit simpler. It was often still a joint of beef but out went the showstoppers, the Yorkshires, the honey-glazed parsnips and in their place, plainer boiled peas with runner beans and carrots with no more than three roast potatoes.

Even though we'd only afforded to do it three times, it had become a sort of October tradition but the beef Wellington was also consigned to history as was anything with a lot of pastry, such as a tarte Tatin, the traditional apple pie and rice puddings or any heavy pudding which had a main ingredient of full-fat cream.

Even my own personal curry had to be modified, one of the Saturday dishes, the coconut block being replaced by zero-fat yoghurt.

We did, however, rediscover the delights of the crumble, a much underrated pudding, easy to make and more versatile than any pie or French style tart.

The immediate diet changes helped stabilize his condition as the collapsing, the shaking and the falling over all stopped from the moment we knew and the diet changed.

I didn't cook for him every day at this stage but it was because of this that we started doing all our shopping together instead of just special shopping trips such as at Christmas.

I used to cycle off very early in the mornings, especially if I had work to do, to get my shopping from our local Tesco, which was open 24 hours a day. I happened to mention how quiet it was between eight and ten and so we started doing our shopping together.

This had started before his diabetes was known to us, before the dark period began, and we used to go up on the Tesco Free Bus.

The first change in 2010 was that the Tesco Free Bus was removed from our estate and we had to use the regular bus. This meant we started to arrive earlier, which in turn meant we had between half an hour and fifty minutes to wait for a bus home and in addition there was the journey time.

As a consequence we started to use the cafe while waiting and, started to buy our frozen foods from Iceland.

At first it was just a drink, then a cake or a sandwich were added, but as we started using the 9:15 bus, we started having brunch there.

You chose what you wanted from an array of breakfast fare displayed in the warming pans and each item was either priced individually, so per rasher of bacon or for each hash brown, or by the spoonful, like mushrooms and baked beans, the staff member serving you and you paying the accumulated cost at the end. It worked out very reasonable and was very good.

When we knew about the diabetes, I encouraged him to have more mushrooms, tomatoes and scrambled egg, and less bacon and sausage, which he did. Scrapping the meal altogether wouldn't have worked as he looked forward to having something and it helped him cope with the whole shopping experience. Only at Christmas time did we not bother as, even at such an early time, the cafe was crowded.

But, coinciding with the dark time and his prolonged relapse, things began to change quickly at the cafe too. Some of the products were changed for cheaper inferior brands and the taste was so noticeable that we started to leave things out of our regular order and make up the difference with mushrooms and beans. Then the drinks dispenser kept breaking down, so more often than not he wasn't getting his cola drink and I couldn't get a coffee and had to have a tea. Sometimes then the mini teapots didn't have a teabag in them and you had to chase up the staff member to let you have one.

There were fewer staff so, instead of someone running the till and one serving, the person out front was stocking up, serving, doing the toast and taking the money. It was becoming such a long process getting the food that we were now in danger of missing our bus and on several occasions we had to almost run with our shopping to make it.

So, after a month, we stopped eating there, only having a drink.

Then Costa took over so we treated ourselves to a breakfast once before shopping but now you couldn't choose what you wanted.

There were set options, four if you didn't count the veggie versions, and the one choice that was for the same price was such a disappointment. Hardly anything on the plate, it didn't taste all that much of anything and unlike our original meals wasn't filling either, meaning we had to eat again at midday instead of going through until four. The only positive of the whole experience was that they gave you a number and brought the food to you so you could sit and wait.

All in all, enough to make anyone depressed.

So we never ate there again.

That in itself wasn't the end of the Tesco shop but the café changes certainly helped and, as we had no reason to be hanging around, we stopped getting the bus back, taking a taxi instead.

As the dark period hit, the anxiety and the paranoid agoraphobia it produced stopped him wanting to go out at all unless he had to. The supermarket run became his only real trip out of the house when he wasn't picking up his pills, so he was doing less and less, even before the taxis home became too expensive and it was cheaper to get the shopping delivered. Then we'd do it online.

Although I kept encouraging him to cut out the sweets, the fizz and so on and he did cut it down to half of the supply, making the rest up with the zero-sugar substitutes, it was a habit too hard to break completely.

He liked to push the trolley so both our loads went in the one trolley and we'd basically follow the store round. As I was now collecting more cook books, our Saturday and Sunday dinners were often included in this shop, except for the joint which Stewart bought the next day in Whitstable. With the diabetes in mind, I was always concerned about the fat, salt and sugar content and I would at times mention it if I saw too many red traffic lights in the trolley.

Sometimes I'd try to talk him out of a product with some success but usually a healthier alternative was the key.

'I need chips.'

'Why don't you get oven chips?'

'Oven chips?' He'd look at me blankly by the cheapest packet of ready-sliced chips you needed to deep fry with half a litre of oil.

'Yeah, they're healthier, less fat.'

He'd pull a face thinking it meant they weren't as good.

'They taste the same and it'll help control your diabetes.'

He thought again for a moment, his tongue sweeping over his lower lip as he did when he was giving something some careful thought.

'It's what I eat,' I would add just then, to sway him.

'Okay then.'

And he'd let me pick the bag and, after a while, the fat fryer ended up having to be thrown away, the old congealed fat inside starting to rot as it was never used again.

Pasta also became part of the staples, originally a spag bol, before moving into the Italian cuisine and to the wonder of herbs.

Little lifestyle changes meant his weight stabilized and his mood brightened. Even in the dark days, he was getting up in the day more often, even if it was still after ten, and he was now drawing his curtains, which meant he could start owning plants and his windowsill was never without a plant again, even if their survival was more hit and miss.

His medication for diabetes was in tablet form and, according to a programme on BBC4, was reversible if you could get your waistline under 42 inches, but we wouldn't see that programme for a couple of years so, to begin with, we were just trying to manage his condition.

We searched online to find a recipe book which we could use for weekend cooking that was diabetic friendly and tried to buy dinners for the week that he could cook himself and would be healthier. So he started to buy Weight Watchers meals, instead of the really cheap ready meals but, apart from their quiche, he didn't really like the taste of them. A couple of days during the week, if he stayed on a quiche and maybe some breaded fish or something, I'd make something else from the recipe books that was healthier than what he would normally have cooked himself.

The first of the new books was a 1970s diabetes diet book from a charity shop and, to be honest, reading some of the recipes you could understand why it was in a charity shop. The food was too bland. But even with all this healthier food and smaller portions, the sugar-free drinks and more fruit and veg, the weight and waistline didn't diminish.

Jamie Oliver was on his healthy food crusade but his recipes were too much work for too little reward. You ended up doing a lot of faffing about in the kitchen, prepping something which tasted no better than the supermarket's own brand version of the same thing as a ready meal and, in the end, I'm not sure actually much healthier than what I cooked on a Saturday before we found out about the diabetes, so we dumped him almost as quickly as we found him as again there was no change to Stewart's waistline.

Antony Worrall Thompson's book for diabetics was better and tasty, though expensive to do on a daily basis, but we kept with him for a couple of months. Then, at the end of 2012 and therefore into 2013, the best book by 'The Hairy Dieters' was published and in that book we virtually tried all the recipes. The best thing about it was it had some of what they called fake-away dinners, curries that sort of thing, but most importantly they tasted good, had a lower calorie count than even the better ready meals and were better value all in all than a Weight Watchers meal. Above all, they made Stewart realise that there was more to a Sunday dinner than just beef and that a curry could be healthy.

He didn't have any more falls or hypoglycaemic comas and cut out the junk food almost completely. It was hard habit for him to break of course as it was something he'd picked up since his labouring days. As a result, we could go to Canterbury occasionally, like to The Game, and not have to have a burger and chips but have a coffee and a sandwich instead, and because the 'Hairy Dieters' menus tasted nice, he didn't feel the need to sneak a cheese roll or a burger puff downtown with a can of coke and a sweet anymore as when the other diets got too much.

7

Before 2010, he would go Canterbury three, four times a year, usually taking me with him, but sometimes he went either with another friend or, as his confidence grew, on his own. I didn't mind going, especially around Christmas time as I would combine the day with a bit of present buying.

Usually we'd go to The Game, taking the old games to sell, then buying some more and a couple of new ones, then burger and chips with a milkshake at Burger King, then home.

Sometimes it would include getting some more trainers or a pair of tracksuit bottoms. We didn't shop online before 2010.

On the whole these trips were uneventful but that's not to say they weren't fun. He wasn't a big talker then so the bus trip was usually quiet. We'd go up to the top deck and watch the scenery. I'd point out some feature in a garden I liked. I like gardens though don't have one. I might get a response but he wouldn't really come out of his thoughts until we reached Canterbury.

He was always in a hurry to get off. I'd hardly stood up when he'd be going down the stairs, to queue for the lower deck to clear. I would sit at the front, by the windows, and he would sit two to three rows back, even if we were the only people on the bus's top deck, and at first I thought this was because he didn't like the sun in his face. I'm always wearing sunglasses so it doesn't bother me but then, after a while, I realized he was always opposite the stairs, the exit route. He had to be able to get to the exit and if on the odd occasion the top deck was busy and he couldn't be that near to the stairs, he'd say,

'I'll see you at the other end. I'm going downstairs.'

'Want me to come down?'

'No, you stay.'

Because of this, when we travelled together and knowing I preferred the upper deck, he would want to leave on the nine fifteen, even when the council changed the bus times for the bus passes starting from nine to half past, the nine fifteen was the one he wanted to be on, because it was after the school kids and before all the pensioners got on the quarter to ten.

So that was the time we always headed off, which meant we'd be in Canterbury by quarter past ten, as we didn't change buses in Whitstable but stayed on the one bus that took us the long way round to the city, I suspect because our bus would be less crowded as the journey went on, but as neither of us were in any particular hurry, it made the journey more of a day out.

Once in the city, all the calm and the relaxation I'd felt on the meandering journey would soon evaporate as his breathing would rise and he seemed to be filled with eager energy but of course, in truth, he was suffering with nervousness.

Apart from the obvious size and location of Canterbury compared to Whitstable, they are both very different towns. However, they do share the same basic layout. The majority of the shops and the focus of the commercial heart of the town are along the central high street but, unlike Whitstable, even when it's crowded and full of tourists, the feel and the mentality of Canterbury is completely different. It's a colder, less friendly place, with everyone rushing about and in too much of a hurry. Even the street vendors seem to be there as little more than a traffic-calming measure, designed to frustrate the regular shopper, and are shouting at you all the time to buy their stuff.

In Whitstable, you got to know the shopkeepers you visited regularly because at this time there weren't as many international big-name stores as there are now and there was a greater variety of shops.

We'd also get to know some of the town's characters in passing and it was easy to strike up a friendly conversation with a stranger and just chat. It felt safer, warmer, and you knew if you did have any troubles, like collapsing in the street, people would come to your aid and not steal your mobile or anything else, which you couldn't say felt true in Canterbury.

Nor was Canterbury just transforming into a large university town, turning old petrol stations, even Clarkson House, into the extended university campus, more classes and more accommodation, but now whole estates were full of transient student residents, such as the Downs Road area, so little by little and very quickly too, the city had gone from what had been a warmer, friendlier place with lots of diverse shops to little more than pubs and cafés. This was in part to encourage the European travellers, who then might send their kids to the university, but largely because, as the demographic make-up of the town changed, instead of people shopping for fish, meat and vegetables in town, the residents were now in their cars shopping at the supermarkets and the tourists and the students were filling up the city, drinking and dining on junk food, neither group in any desperate need to go and buy a fish.

Coupled with the noise and people in their own personal mindsets, barging their way through, it used to make me feel uneasy, compared to safe old Whitstable, so I could empathise just how hard it was for him and why he always wanted to get out of there as soon as possible, almost as soon as the bus doors closed and we stepped off into the depot.

By the time I'd stepped off the bus, he'd be already in the shelter, worried expression on his face, looking for me, and as I came over, he'd turn ready to go as I reached him.

'Where do you want to go to first?' I'd say.

'The Game.'

'Do you want to get a coffee or something first?'

'No,' and we'd already be across the road approaching Fenwick's.

The Game was often busy but with a different set of busy people, the enthusiast. Now I can relate to standing around flicking through endless titles, reading the backs of them and trying to think if you'd like it or not, as in my youth I'd spend just as much time at various record shops doing just that with row upon row of cassettes and vinyl, wondering which I should buy.

But Stewart didn't do any of that.

His first mission was to find the new version of the football game, which he'd find without much effort as if he had homing radar for it. Then another new game, usually car-based, would be next.

He'd then look at the second-hands for sale and pick a few. He knew what his budget was and would continue choosing games until he had the budget spent, and that included the money back on the old games he'd traded in.

Then with them bagged up and put in his rucksack, it would be off to get whatever I needed and sometimes some food shopping too but, more often than not, as it would be around midday by now, we'd head off to find somewhere to eat.

Before we knew about the diabetes, he was a big burger fan, so the only place to go was Burger King, for two reasons. The Burger King in town was an older place, not part of the redevelopment and smaller, less of a draw for teenagers, than McDonalds.

We had tried McDonalds the first time we'd visited the city together but they'd changed their decoration, crammed more tables into the upstairs section and bolted the chairs down, all of which made it an uncomfortable experience, so we never went back. Burger King for those early years became the place to go.

But it was because of an incident on one visit, ironically the last time we went to The Game and the last time we went to Canterbury that wasn't for any government-related business or Christmas, that we never went into any burger place in the city again.

It had been a strange day all round and not part of our normal routine. I had a dentist check-up at around twelve, he had wanted to go to The Game and we'd decided to mix the two trips into the one day. He hadn't wanted to wait at my surgery so I had left him in a nearby café. After getting the all clear, I'd joined him twenty minutes later, had a coffee as he had another drink and then we'd made our way up through the main heart of the city towards the store.

As is always the case, towards the bus station it gets busier and more congested as everyone else seems to be coming down and I noticed his anxiety levels rising as we made our way to the store but, once inside, he seemed to calm down and everything was fine.

He got his games and we then went to the Burger King.

A different time of day, it was now nearer two and a busier hour, the lower half of the restaurant was crowded and, as it was a chilly day, eating it in the nearby Dane John wasn't an option so we had to go upstairs, something we'd never done before.

I carried the tray and halfway up, coming down were three teenage lads in school uniform and as they passed us, one quipped for his friends to hear though we heard too,

'Wouldn't it be fun to tip the tray out of his hands?'

Typical me, the only thought to pass through my mind then was 'arsehole' and even then I was probably promoting him above his intelligence grade. However, when we reached our table and as I was passing Stewart his food, I noticed he was looking angry.

'Like to hit that idiot in the head.'

'He's just showing off to his mates. It's what teens do, try and boast about things. Just ignore them. They're not worth it.'

'I know... Still.'

'Eat your burger.'

He fumed about it for the rest of the day. But I got the impression that it wasn't the teenagers that were the reason behind his anger. There was something deeper to it, something in his past, the way he'd been treated when younger by his birth parents was probably the underlining factor here. Teens being stupid wasn't an uncommon occurrence and not something that would normally make him react other than maybe with a disappointed shake of the head.

There was a bitterness there and though he never talked about his biological family, only his foster parents, Sue and Graham, whom he would call mum and dad, I felt that incident had opened up and old wound.

I won't dwell on it any further, partly because that wasn't him. He wasn't full of bitterness and partly, well, his biological parents don't deserve the cost of the ink in printing anything about them.

He was a gentle soul and stupidity like that would be one of the few occasions he would express a suppressed anger. I would struggle to count even on one hand the amount of times he was ever angry. It would more likely be something on the news that would annoy him, such as when the state oversaw injustices and was caught covering things up. Those things often brought out a response, but genuine anger, no.

But we never went to The Game again, or to Burger King or shopping together in Canterbury other than for Christmas ever again. When he did buy new computer games, they were always old ones from the charity shops and, by 2011, we weren't playing computer games together anymore.

8

He was also the only person I've ever met who would do something for a friend without the inducement of a reward or expecting you to do them a favour afterwards in exchange for the original favour. In a way, it was also an attitude that caused him more pain than it needed to as he was often reluctant to ask for help until the problem was a lot bigger than it needed to be.

This wouldn't change really until around 2015 but before then life wasn't too much of a struggle. Everything was going fine and I could rely on him as much as he could rely on me.

I'd gone to B&Q to get some compost for my indoor plants, only to find that there was a deal on two bags bigger than the one I wanted that would give me more than double the compost for cheaper than the original bag. No brainer, that was the deal to buy, only I didn't have a car and couldn't get them both on the bike.

The bus was the perfect option. It stopped outside Stewart's door and we could catch it only a few hundred yards away from B&Q. I asked Stew if he'd come with me the next day to pick up the bags and he agreed.

When we arrived in Chestfield, I surprised him by buying him a KFC Burger with coke and fries as a treat for helping me out, and without hinting I was going to do so beforehand, before we went and got my compost.

He was genuinely surprised and was so made up that he had a happy mood for the rest of the day. The compost was heavy, even heavier by the time we reached the stop, and what was normally a ten-minute walk took twenty, but we made it alright.

Because he was often reluctant to ask for help until the last minute, sometimes this had comic consequences.

The old washing machine had broken down and needed replacing. A new one was ordered and all that had to be done was to disconnect the old one and move it out from under the sink unit so the new one could be slotted in and the old one taken away as the store directed.

I went round. I was going to help him drag the old one out and was having a cup of tea first as Stewart decided to clear the space under the sink to get to the water pipe.

'I'll be with you in a minute.'

'Alright.' I heard his muffled reply echo back to me.

'Need a hand?' Hoping he'd say no, as I didn't fancy taking all the cleaning stuff out from off the shelf.

'No.'

So I was drinking my tea when suddenly there was a cry. I came rushing in and there was water everywhere. Stewart was trying to hold the jet of water back and in an instant I was over and turned the tap, just behind where the water pipe to the machine had been connected to the main supply, to the off position.

'Forgot to turn the water off.'

'No shit, Sherlock!' I replied as both of us, now soaked, stood in a kitchen that resembled a swimming pool.

It took us an hour to clear it up before we could move the machine and after a cup of tea, we both started to laugh about it.

'What am I like?' he'd asked, upturning the palms of his hands as he asked the question and then he'd proceeded to tell his parents what had happened.

However, the next day when the new one arrived, the floor was so clean and polished, that the new one glided easily into place. This time, the tap was turned after the pipe was firmly in place.

Yet apart from playing the games, particularly the football, and a bit of telly, he was still largely a quiet person, who constantly looked as if there was a large weight on his mind and he was waiting to be disappointed.

I would say, 'Don't worry. It might never happen.'

He'd say, 'But what if it does?'

I'd say, 'If it does, it's too late to worry about it. It's happened.'

He'd just grunt as if he knew it was coming.

Then it did.

9

When my grandparents died, though I did get a bit depressed during that time, I never lost sight of myself because Stewart being around, being just his normal self and being able to just let me talk to him about them on occasions when I needed an outlet, was the rock I needed to come to terms with losing the first people in my life that had been close to me.

He would listen and not suddenly hijack the conversation to then talk about anyone in his family that might have died, like some 'other friends' would do, as if we were playing a game of 'death top trumps'. He helped me get through. As all my family are well scattered across the UK, it would have been a much more difficult time without him being there.

However bad those two events may have been for me, for him, 2010 to 2012, if I hadn't been there, might well have been the end of him as the evil empire took over and had this amazing brainwave that people with long-term welfare needs were too expensive to be kept.

To be honest, it almost sounded like the Nuremberg Rallies all over again and it seemed that with a new T-4 programme, the evil empire had imported a group of pen pushers with no real medical background to assess Stewart and send him back to work.

I say with good evidence that they had no knowledge of what they were doing as the questions and tests they devised to assess him by were for his physical condition, like could he walk ten metres unaided, could he raise his arms, which anyone with a brain cell will tell you aren't prerequisite problems for a mental disease. In fact, it's quite the reverse, as you can have a mental disease without any outward afflictions whatsoever.

I went with him to the assessment meeting at Nutwood House (apply named but it's to do with the author of Rupert the Bear, Mary Tourtel, who was from Canterbury, and not the required entry level of IQ or abilities of the assessment staff) but they wouldn't let me in the room with him. The questions and the assessment were all about getting welfare numbers down, not assessing a person's needs. If there had been two doors, one leading to a shower block, it wouldn't have been a surprise, as their assessment was pernicious and evil.

Heading home, he told me the questions were like,

'Can you walk more than ten metres without getting out of breath, can you talk to a person over the phone, can you catch a bus and can you pay a bill?'

Well, he was overweight, but anyone can pay a bill these days, it's called direct debit, but that wasn't the condition that was stopping him working. He'd got mental issues not physical ones, numbnuts, and was why his GP had signed him off in the first place.

The fact he'd turned up without being able to drive proved he could catch a bus. The fact I was with him because he couldn't do an unfamiliar journey on his own, which they didn't ask, showed he had anxiety issues which they dismissed. The same went for the telephone. If he had a problem and needed to contact someone, he'd try and sort it on his own at first but often he would get confused and frustrated and just hang up. The biggest fault of those systems was he'd tell them the problem but they'd be reading a computer's script and he would get annoyed with them then asking the very questions which he'd already answered. So he would have me sort it out for him instead.

Taking on a service, like a Sky TV bundle for example, by phone is easy. All they want is your name, address and how you're going to pay. When the system goes down and you need to explain why it's not working or you have to follow instructions about something you don't understand, given to you by a person with a strong, non-

Kentish accent, and that's another matter. No one in their right mind would have given Stewart a job at that time and his anxiety and paranoia problems in unfamiliar settings would have made his condition worse.

With that and his care funding also ending halfway through all this, just as the pressure was reaching its height, the poor guy was isolated against a hostile regime who wanted to destroy his very way of life.

During this time, before the care was withdrawn, Stewart started self-harming and the solution his carer came up with was confiscating all his knives, which for a few months meant I had to come round on a Sunday with my own set of knives so we could have dinner.

It also meant he became reliant on takeaway food and ready-made meals, anything that didn't need a knife to prepare it basically, which probably aided and accelerated his diabetes problems. So in trying to save money, they'd actually added more to the NHS bill as his medicine intake increased. You go figure!

When the carer was gone, he overdid his medication a couple of times, though he never had enough fortunately to do any damage. His GP noticed on one of his check-ups that the 'counts' were irregular and he ending up being put on a seven-day prescription, which he remained on thereafter and had to have his schizophrenia medication dosage strength increased.

For a while, this left him in a bit of a daze at times or he was so distraught by what was happening to him that he didn't care, listening to his demons instead, and he started to just suddenly cross roads without looking in either direction first.

When I was with him, I could stop him, often grabbing him by the shoulder as well as calling to him not to cross. But twice at least to my knowledge, he was down in the town and just suddenly crossed the road, only to be hit by a car, once actually knocked to the floor, but in both cases, there was nothing broken and he wasn't concussed. He just picked himself up and carried on.

If things hadn't changed, and if I hadn't been there, I'm sure he would have killed himself during those dark days. During those two years, it did actually happen that two people were run down and killed, just suddenly stepping out into traffic, and even a shop front was damaged, not counting the poor guy who hung himself in his flat.

Before his benefits were cut and he was forced to go to the Jobcentre once a month, he had well-managed accounts, in as much his income and outgoings all fitted in with his benefit payments and what was left he spent on food, heating and so on.

Well, the change in benefit dates, the loss of a lot of the money and falling behind with payments, soon meant he was in debt, and instead of talking to anyone about it, he tried to cover the gap with a doorstep loan, which plugged the gap to start with, but when the next month's demands came in, he had them plus the loan to cover and it all became too much. He defaulted, started to incurred monthly bank charges, until they stopped honouring his direct debits and then he turned to me to help him.

Problem was it didn't stop there. He became timid around people and if you live on the poor side of the tracks, you're easy prey to the evil firms with their simple terms and high interest rates.

They would either phone or come round in person, badger him, often not let him get a word in edgeways, on and on about how wonderful their scheme was, and at a time with the added stress eating away at him, so much so that he just really wanted to be left alone and hide. He didn't have the will to say no and, like too many vulnerable people, which is why they're targeted in the first place, he was signed up to more deals, different power companies, that sort of thing. If he'd had a carer to look after him, they would have spotted all this sooner as they would have been checking things like his letters and all these things could have been avoided but because I wouldn't see him until the evening, I wouldn't know about some daytime hawkers calling until he couldn't cope.

I contacted those concerned and helped him get onto a managed repayment scheme. For a while we stopped paying the water bills by direct debit and started to pay by card. It meant as his money came in, we'd work out what bills had to be paid and then the rest was 'his' money.

We junked the Sky TV and everything else and to his credit, even though once his debt was cleared and all these companies tried to sign him up again, from then on it was just Freeview and broadband for the house phone and so we could do our online shopping.

All of that had sent him back into a deep depression. His self-loathing and the morbid desire to end it all were back and instead of getting up around half nine to half ten in the morning, most times when I'd come round, for eighteen months, he'd still be in bed and at that time, I was still coming round about four to five in the afternoon after I'd had dinner. I noticed once coming back from the Co-op as it now was, after I'd left his to get some milk for the next day, so it would have been nearly ten at night, his flat was already dark. He was only getting out of bed because I was coming round, every day now, and only from the time I was there.

He had an extreme preoccupation with religion and the occult, watching horror films based around those subjects and had started to buy more and more slash-horror movies, to a point where he had over two hundred of them. His carer's only solution had been to tell him not to buy any and once or twice she made him get rid of them but he only bought them back again from the charity shops.

He didn't want to play the computer games anymore and he became more withdrawn, to the point where I was the only person he ever saw for months, outside of his GP or the pharmacist.

I would say something like,

'What did you do today?'

'Nothing.'

'Didn't you sit out front?'

'No.'

'But it was a nice sunny day. Why not?'

'Why?'

'Why' became the answer to almost any question.

'Would you set the tables for dinner, knives, forks and spoons.'

'Why?'

'Because I'm cooking the bloody thing and if you don't want to use chopsticks or your fingers, set the bloody table.' I'm no Ainsley Harriott, more your Keith Floyd with a hint of Gordon Ramsey when creating a three-course meal from scratch.

'Alright then.'

Strangely, I never got angry about anything, frustrated at times maybe and I didn't make allowances for his condition. That is to say, I understood why certain things wouldn't or didn't happen but I wasn't going to pander to them, so in a way my attitude and my behaviour around him didn't change whether he was in a good place or a bad place, which I think helped as he knew I was always going to be a constant in his life.

But it was a dark time, of mostly lows those years. He hardly smiled, he hardly laughed and it was a struggle to get him interested in anything whatsoever.

He just wanted to stay in bed all day.

I did start coming round earlier, three in the afternoon, so he at least did see some daylight, but he was often too deep inside himself to be interested in anything even then.

Partly he felt punished for being honest or maybe being honest confirmed to him that he had no self-worth, because although he'd answered their questions correctly, they were taking all his safety net, his world, away and threatening to force him into a situation where it was clear he couldn't cope.

The sleepless nights, the anxiousness and increased paranoia were all down to this. It got to a point where he'd lie to people, especially over the phone to people like his parents, to give them the answer he thought they wanted to hear, rather than tell the truth in fear that they might not call him again.

Feeling that everyone around him was judging him, he found it difficult to go out and after a while even going to the supermarket to get food was difficult, though all this strangely coincided with home delivery becoming cheaper as the taxi prices when up, so we did at least ensure that he would have a well-stocked freezer but, as the depression gripped, he began to drink more and more cola.

To try and get him out more, we started getting our Sunday joint from Rooks and all our meals we had together were made from fresh ingredients from scratch.

We also cut down his desire for self-destruction with alcohol as he'd started to buy cheap lager and spirits. He wasn't yet drinking on an alcoholic's scale, just a beer a day, but he could drink half a bottle of rum with coke in a night, albeit once a month rather than every night. It was a reaction to when he was at his lowest ebb and as someone who wasn't a drinker who could also go for months without a single drop, when he did drink, it was a big reaction.

So by getting top quality wine to go with Sunday dinner, the sort where one glass, not one bottle, is enough and starting to have beers only with live football matches and special events, which as Sky took over the world, dwindled down to England games mostly.

Sunday dinner was a lot of work for me in the kitchen and at that time he wasn't able to help in any way as the depression often meant all he would do was climb out of bed as I arrived and then lie on the sofa watching repeats of Columbo until I dished up, only getting up to do the washing up, which I would refuse to do, but some of it would be left until the following weekend, only being washed up properly the next time I needed that pot or pan.

The irony was, those in real need the evil empire was abandoning and those not really needing state help so badly but smart enough to play the system were doing whatever it took to ensure they kept what they'd got. One guy I know went to the interview on crutches and by taxi, not because he couldn't walk unaided or use a bus. His condition was largely a back problem which had stopped him doing his old job as a window cleaner and the state had never seen fit to train him for something else he could do instead. But he ended up with extra benefits because of 'his condition' and Stewart had to fight to get what he deserved.

And in any case the plans didn't work. After reducing staffing, reducing benefits, reducing and closing Outreach and Help Centres, they saved so little and had still added and added to the original national debt without ridding us of the deficit. As a result the country began to creak and break up so they had to start spending again and start putting it all back, announcing the introduction of more training to bring in more staff, spending more on mental health care. Even the Royals gave back some of their public money to fund a mental health charity and to look at bringing more help into the community.

Only took those seven years and a huge rise in funding.

But through those dark days, during the week he wouldn't eat anything other than snack food for weeks on end, only getting a decent meal if I cooked it and all his thoughts were dark. He didn't joke or mess about and for the most part it was like being with the living dead. It seemed there was really no way in to his mind.

Even things that he had loved, like football and Formula 1, let us down. England couldn't get out of the group stages, even letting goals dribble through the keeper's legs, and F1, after the first bend of the second lap, unless a car's engine blew up, which only seemed to happen in the movies, the order they were in was the order they finished and if you want to see cars travelling in a procession for two hours, it's cheaper and slightly more entertaining to stand on a motorway bridge.

So he was getting bored.

This only made the depression worse.

The second sofa for a while became a bit of a dumping ground for things like old magazines and cushions. He bought a lot of cushions and soft toys from the local charity shop and filled both sofas with the toys across the tops against the wall. It was the more obvious start of his space-filling obsession which began in earnest during the dark times.

That's not to say he hadn't been doing that already but then he'd only moved onto the estate a few months before me, so until now his space filling was little different to mine in as much as he was setting down roots, but now it seemed he was making up for lost time.

Soft toys ended up on the shelving on top of the DVDs and it was around now that he started to raid the charity shops for DVDs, no matter what the title was, buying more and more, at first to fill the shelves, then in piles on the floor, anywhere in the lounge it seemed and around 'his half' of the room as if he was making a fortress around himself.

This behaviour would continue until then end of 2015.

Fortunately, I was there to support him and his GP, the only qualified professional in all of this by the way, put herself out big time to ensure not just that his benefits were restored with backpay but also that he didn't have to then sign on or look for work and by 2012 he was beginning to come back out of his shell a bit more and get his life in order.

After a few weeks, he did start to take some interest in things. It would be his task to go and buy the meat on his own on a Wednesday. We'd buy the rest of it together the day after, but he'd choose the joint and, although for one whole year, we had beef for nearly every Sunday dinner, at least he was getting up, going out and doing something worthwhile.

By the start of 2013, he was back to his old 2009 self.

However, the damage was done. He may not have been so depressed anymore but instead was now suffering a mania that would haunt him for the rest of his life.

10

Even after his GP had forced the issue and his life was sorted out again, it took us all that time just to get him back to how he was before this rubbish all began and it would still be another year before he was out of his deep depression and two before he would be debt free again.

It was also the moment my life changed when friendship won, as a long business frustration that had plagued me for the most part of 2011 was resolved, along with another offer, and I had the chance to take my business into the big league, only with Stewart in such a dark place then, I was placed in a bit of a dilemma.

As his carer was now gone and he was still somewhat fragile mentally due to the scars of the evil empire, I was now the only person he turned to if he had a significant problem and though everything was now under control, his confidence was totally shot away. He would come back from taking the rubbish out to the wheelie bin with all the symptoms of an anxiety attack.

I had all I needed to begin but no firm start date and with the thought of leaving him alone for what would be the best part of a year, it didn't seem right to go now, six weeks before Christmas when he was still so fragile and needed stability and routine in his life. He was a friend in need and, anyway, I could postpone until the New Year, thinking it would only be six weeks.

Only things didn't work quite as I thought and six weeks would turn into six years, with me not really picking up where I'd left off until January 2017.

But how do you get someone with no interest in anything, not even themselves, interested in something again.

Movies helped. He even joined the supermarket's mailing list, renting DVDs for a couple of years and we started to watch films of all different genres, action, comedy, art-house and so on. We'd choose ten each from the list of available titles and after a month, and we'd seen a few, we'd add a few more.

For a little while it worked fine but we decided to end the subscription when we weren't getting to see the new releases we really wanted and on some occasions we received fewer discs than we should have as no others on our list were available and his impatience meant he went and bought it instead.

But the thing I think helped most to break his introspective cycle and which was most effective came about by chance and was all about answering the phone.

At that time, I had a friend who would ring me once a month on a Thursday and we'd meet up on a Saturday morning and then I'd go round to Stewart's after our normal time. Over this dark period, I had my phone on me as I was visiting Stewart daily and that from then on never changed, so more often than not I'd receive this call at Stewart's and I noticed after a couple of occasions coming back into the lounge how Stew would ask me a question or two about the call.

Maybe he was worried we were talking about him. The fact was, though I had always told my parents about Stew, which I had always told Stewart I did, and on a few occasions I had talked to them at his place, my phone-calling friend and I only got together to watch old TV shows whilst eating take-away fish and chips and he'd only talk about himself anyway. I seldom got a word in to talk about myself as it was, so even if I had wanted to talk about Stewart, I couldn't have, so we didn't.

Now our mutual friend Mark, who at this time I really only met when he visited Stewart once every couple of months, knew about Stewart's diabetes and depression and wanted to help.

He would come round to see Stewart at Christmas when I was

away but on the whole Stew knew him better than I did. They had known each other and been friends for five years before I had first ever met him back in the YMCA.

Mark liked sport and was always playing snooker on Saturdays with Jasper at the Catholic Club or tennis at Swalecliffe, so when Mark came round one time, that October, I suggested we all do a shared activity and they both seemed up for it. Stewart, I will admit, a little begrudgingly but he was by now getting up again at around ten or eleven so his moods were improving.

I thought swimming was a good way to keep fit and Whitstable's got a great pool. Okay I can swim but it's been a long time so I wasn't expecting to be able to do fifty lengths. I thought maybe a couple of lengths and a bit of floating, a good way to kill an hour.

Also I thought it would help Stewart to both build his confidence and lose some weight to help manage his diabetes, the state-enforced depression having made him gain weight.

The idea was we'd cycle down, swim for twenty minutes and talk and bob around for the rest of the hour you get, but then the plan was scuppered because Mark couldn't swim and Stewart was worried about what people might think as he couldn't swim either and was also worried about what other people might think of his appearance.

I could sympathise with that. Also we would have to go quite early in the morning or else we'd have ended up with the mothers and toddlers or the crowds in the evenings but the idea to do something, once a month, just the three of us was sound.

Next door to the pool is a ten-pin bowling alley and so I suggested that.

Crown bowls would have been next as that's nearby too but I'm not sure you can borrow the woods so it might have been too expensive to try and, after meeting some of the people who play that sport, it seemed a bit too cutthroat and all too serious to me. I can't imagine you could bowl with an end wood in one hand and a pint in the other and, to my mind, if you can't do that, then it's all way too serious.

Fortunately, they both agreed so we planned there and then to go bowling.

It was Mark that pointed out the obvious. How we could arrange the times and so forth? It was again my suggestion he should call

Stewart, as Mark already had his number and Stew and I would be travelling down together. Stew would be able to tell me if anything changed and he could keep Mark up to date.

As a result, he was now the all-important hub for all our group activities. Mark would ring on a Sunday to see if we all wanted to go bowling, I'd agree to book it on the Tuesday and Stewart would ring Mark once it was done, with Mark ringing again on the Thursday to check everything was still okay. Eventually, as his confidence grew, Stewart would end up ringing Mark every day from that Tuesday to remind him to be there on that Friday.

We both travelled down by bus the very first time and all three of us played. At that time I thought it was best to go for the early-bird sessions, which started after eleven, but I arranged it for two in the afternoon. That way we'd be back at his by half four and we were having a chilli for dinner.

At that time of day, we could guarantee hardly anyone else would be there, and for the most part this was true. More often than not, the OAP set would be leaving and apart from maybe parents with pre-school children out for the day and the odd loved-up teens, six to eight of the ten lanes we could guarantee would be empty.

We turned up, got our three-tone shoes from behind the counter and then started our first game, barriers down always, and though we each guttered more than our fair share, it was fun. We had a soft drink as we played and a coffee after and, within eight points of each other, we all managed to reach scores well into the sixties.

We played air hockey afterwards, which Stewart really liked, and planned to do it again in two weeks. So I re-booked there and then.

The improvement wasn't immediate, as he did regress a few times over the next year and there were times when we booked the lane and I would ride down alone, with Stewart coming by bus later. In that first year of bowling sometimes he wouldn't show, wouldn't answer the phone when we tried to find out if he was coming and we had to just make it the two of us that day.

When he did join us again, he found himself left behind a bit as our game was improving, but getting him out, getting him involved and getting some enthusiasm into his life was what he needed, and so, as a compromise, to take the pressure off and to encourage him to join us more, I said to him,

'As long as you come, you don't have to play if you don't want to. We're happy to let you watch and if you do want to join in, that's fine too. Just come that's all.'

From then on he came, always missing the bus that would get him there on time, but would be there, fifteen minutes into the game, but never again did he miss a bowling afternoon.

We'd be playing, talking about life in general and then, almost like clockwork, we'd spy him coming in and taking up a seat, by the rail, in front of our lane.

Mark would more often than not buy the three of us a can of something and when it wasn't our turn, we'd spend a bit of time just chatting generally with Stew. When the game was over, the three of us would find a table, have our coffees or hot chocolate, chat for a few minutes before we'd take it in turns to play air hockey.

He enjoyed watching and seeing who was winning and playing the air hockey afterwards. He even on occasion in the warmer months cycled down with me but still didn't play, even though we asked him. He just enjoyed being there with us and getting out from those four walls. The walking from bus stop to bowling alley and the longer distance to town to catch the bus back was at least getting him some exercise which was the point of it all in the first place. The how didn't matter. It was the end result that counted.

As a result, he started once again to go to town more often on his own and it was about then that he started his love of going round the charity shops, bringing back dust gatherers to fill any empty shelf space he had in the flat.

He started to feel more like a valued member of a team but crowds and the anxiety they caused him still determined if he enjoyed the day and that was the one element we couldn't always control.

On a couple of occasions the bowling alley was packed. It was more like a Saturday evening session as, when the summer holidays started, the place was crammed with schoolchildren and sometimes during term time, a school trip from France would see half the place packed out with twenty or so noisy teens, chatting away in a strange language. No fun for a guy who was worried about what people thought about him, with paranoia and anxiety issues. You could see those startled eyes, the withdrawn demeanour and the all tightened-up expression and hear the heavy breath. It wasn't because they were French or children, but it was the noise and the number and the demons in his head telling him, when they laughed, they were laughing at him.

In truth, I doubt any of them noticed him any more than they noticed Mark and me but when you could see the sheer panic in his eyes and the rigid way he stared in our direction as we played. We knew there would be no more bowling during the summer holidays and so after that first year, we never booked a lane during the school holiday periods, always trying to avoid when it was busy.

11

That first week in December of 2012 and for every year after that we would have our Christmas do, which would always start with bowling and then off to the pub.

We decided to go to The Peter Cushing, a Wetherspoon's, which as it turned out, Stewart adored because it's quiet, no loud music, which meant he could talk with us, we wouldn't have to shout to be heard and there are seating areas to the sides which were more secluded, away from prying eyes, and the bar staff just serve you without all that friendly banter.

Initially our Christmas drink was just that. We bought each other a drink and then wished each other 'Happy New Year' before going, in Stewart's and my case, with a slight stagger to the nearby bus stop, for Mark, a bike ride home.

We repeated that the next year but the next three Christmases we'd have something to eat as well. It was Stewart's idea to make it more of an occasion. He sprung it on us by buying the turkey dinner that first time, Mark brought the sweet and I a second round, and that became our Christmas tradition, bowling followed by drinks and a meal at The Peter Cushing, with Mark cycling home after and we'd keep our fingers crossed we'd not missed the six forty-five, as the last bus would be an hour later.

The bowling alley idea had worked, not quite as you'd have imagined, but because of it, he was getting out more, he was getting more mobile and his confidence was improving. He would go to town more often and if someone talked to him, instead of trying to ignore them, he was now, if a little bit gruffly, actually having a conversation with them.

Since the first 'do', he started to become enthusiastic about Christmas, in that by mid-November he would hang, or rather I would hang as he passed them up to me, some decorations across the ceiling. He'd often wanted to put them up the first moment the Christmas items started to appear in the shops, but I would refuse point blank to help put them up before the first Saturday of November.

For a while he did have a tree until the cat started pulling it over. So if it couldn't be hung off the ceiling or on the wall, out of the cat's reach, it didn't go up. Come December, the whole flat would have a very festive feel about it.

He also started writing cards, originally for family and neighbours. I'd write them for us both but I insisted he wrote the one to me and to Mark himself.

It was then, 2013, when we started buying Christmas presents for each other. At first, I thought it was probably a bad idea and set the limit at £10. My experience of buying presents for friends, even girlfriends when you hardly know them, is that it's a dangerous one, as you only know an aspect of what a person likes, through your shared interests. So as long as it's kept within a budget and it's more about the exchange of gifts and what that symbolises rather than what the gift itself is, then it should be fine. Problem is, after a year or three, you start to run out of ideas and the whole thing usually fizzles out.

So I had a bit of trepidation about starting this. A pint down the pub seemed a better idea. In fact, one ex-friend and I used to do just that and it was more fun until he brought presents into the mix, influenced by some woman at work apparently, and within a couple of years, he was history.

Strangely though, this didn't happen to Stewart and me. Originally the present budget meant it was easy and for the first couple of years, we both sort of stuck to it, and I bought him a DVD and he got me something more practical but nothing offensive.

He used to ask,

'What would you like?'

and to take the pressure off I would say,

'Whatever you like, keep within budget and just get something you think I would like.' And for a while he kept to the more generic gifts shops package as gifts for such situations.

But when he started to buy DVDs himself and became compelled to buy them at the charity shops too, a DVD for Christmas wasn't such a good idea, as I couldn't guarantee he wouldn't buy it for himself between me wrapping it and the day itself.

So began us buying things for each other that both went over the initial budget, the first and only person outside my family which I've done this for, and the moment we both started thinking outside the box.

He brought me an electric toothbrush, an expensive razor, a nutcracker with display dish in wood and for our last Christmas, a very nice lasagne dish, which I suspect was just under the £10 limit so he topped it up with some small items too, including a 'Minion soap on a rope'.

For him, the change in direction had meant things like decorative 'Ace of Spades' dust caps for his cruiser bike, an MP3 player with plug-in speakers, though he bought some better over-the-ear earphones later so he could listen to it on the bus, some Balti dishes with naan plate and chutney bowls for curry nights, and a wristwatch. The one which seemed to be the biggest surprise for him was the hamper, a wicker basket, which we later used for our picnics and, as I told him, would be right to use to carry his lunch when he started fishing again. Inside the hamper I'd put some luxury foods as well as some of his much loved favourites, so it had cheeses, chutney, a small port and a wine, shortbread biscuits, some chocolates, a Christmas cake and things like that, which I admit I expected him to have over the Christmas holiday but instead he waited until I came back so we could have the bits and pieces together.

Five Christmases, each one better than before and each now with surprises.

Going to the trouble of thinking about and getting something practical, useful and yet something I didn't have made shopping for a Christmas present fun for him and, as he wasn't trying to be funny or clever or to impress but was thinking what I would like, it meant even the filler objects he'd come up with were right.

He also appreciated the effort almost to a point where he seemed surprised anyone would bother to try so hard. His parents would ask him what he wanted, so he knew what their gift would be, and he would get them the same thing every year too, so there was nothing to Christmas before we started doing this. No magic, no event, other than a settled routine. Even the television had become predictable to a point where you almost didn't have to buy the seasonal listings magazine if you'd kept the one from the year before.

But now, it was an adventure. When he was down the shops, he was looking and thinking what would make a good present. Also, not knowing what I had bought him, as I wouldn't tell him no matter how much he badgered me, meant come the day itself he had a surprise waiting which made the whole day an event and magical. He would ring me almost immediately after opening it and it was in every case a genuine welcome surprise. You could hear it in his voice and it was as if he couldn't believe his luck and all for what? Twenty or so quid.

But his zeal for celebration didn't stop there as we also began to celebrate Halloween. We didn't go in for the parties or 'trick or treat', so no tubs of sweets for the little monsters, but we did buy a couple of pumpkins, which I hollowed out and carved and we lit them, burning tea-lights inside with their faces staring out across the gardens to the flats opposite.

I made us a pumpkin pie and a pecan pie for that first Halloween, but he didn't like the taste of pumpkin, so for the other years, I kept the flesh to use in a savoury pie I enjoyed. However, with those pumpkins and a couple of decorations he found down the charity shop, as well as some animated decorations from the supermarkets, a special dinner, with beer, a toffee apple and a comic horror film, such as 'Ghostbusters', or a clever film like, 'The Craft', we celebrated All Hallows' Eve in our own style.

Having all our group phone calls routed via Stewart also made him more confident using the phone. He still had trouble with accents, so occasionally he would pass them over to me, but that was something like twice in four years. By 2016, he could even order a taxi without my help. And so, after our first Christmas do, he began the daily phone call, in fact not just to Mark, but to his parents and me.

Suddenly he had a way of contacting those who mattered to him without having to wait to see them and he had, in his mind, a legitimate reason to ring and 'Not be a nuisance', in his words not mine.

He would tell his parents about the Christmas presents, what I was up to and the bowling, tell me about what his extended family were up to and keep Mark updated too.

He would even ring me just as I'd got home after seeing him, to find out if I'd made it back home okay. As I never took my phones around to his in those last six years, the fact I was answering the phone was evidence I had and what can befall a person on a five-minute walk on an empty estate I don't know. Or he'd ring a few minutes later or early the next day to check on something we'd already agreed to do, or the funniest one, sometimes the call would go,

'What's up, Stew?'

'Just ringing up for a chat.'

'Okay.'

Silence.

'What you want to talk about?'

Silence.

'The Avengers last night was good, wasn't it?'

'Yeah, it's good to see something we've not seen before even if it is sixty years old.'

Or it would go,

'Everything alright, Stew?'

'Just ringing for a chat.'

'Sure.'

'What you doing?'

'Just finishing off some paperwork,'

'Oh.'

Silence.

'Was thinking, if it's good this Friday, you want to cycle down to the bench, have a picnic or something?'

'Okay.'

Silence.

'Do you want to see if Mark's free too?'

'Okay.'

'Right then, I'll see you at two.'

'Okay.'

Then ten minutes later he'd tell me if Mark was free and it would either be the three of us or just the two of us going for a little picnic.

I even had to move my working day hours forward so when he would ring in the day and say,

'Come round for tea.'

I could say,

'You coming here, or do you want me to come over there?'

'Come round.'

'There.'

'Yeah.'

'Okay.... I'll be about five minutes.'

And the tea would be being made as I'd arrive.

Or he'd ring in the early afternoon.

'Is it alright if I come round for a coffee?'

And unless I needed to finish something by that day, the answer would be, 'Alright then. Can you give me ten minutes to pack away?'

'Okay.'

Then I'd have five minutes as that was one thing that would never change. No two clocks or watches in Stewart's pad ever told the same time. He was a bit like Gomez Addams with his watches as they were often within ten minutes, five either way, of the actual time, but, depending on which clock he wanted to look at, he'd more often than not be around quicker than agreed as he'd checked a second clock and seen what time that one was giving him, leaving when one of them gave him the time he wanted it to be.

Time to Stewart was a fluid thing.

Within a year, he was beginning to be happier; he even started making quips again. He was finding fun in more things, he was getting chatty, wanting to do things, as long as he could get back by seven, and was even beginning to think about making plans for the future.

12

In the summer of 2013 he decided he wanted to be like Mark and me and start cycling. The initial idea was that on a hot summer's day, we could cycle over to Herne Bay and meet over there instead of Mark coming to us all the time.

His impatience meant he wasn't going to save up for one but buy it with that week's disability benefit and bought a cheap mountain bike from the supermarket with his weekly shop.

It was junk.

He had to pedal like a demented hamster to make the thing go and, though it was supposed to have 18 gears, at best he only ever got three out of it. In the end after a couple of rides to the bowling alley and one trip to Swalecliffe, the bike was chucked to the back of the box room, to be buried under the recycling rubbish awaiting its week for collection.

He did want to ride as the next year he mentioned it again, just as the summer was ending, as a couple of times that year, the three of us had gone for a walk along the sea front after bowling, or from his flat past all the beach-front houses until the sea wall began and he'd enjoyed these excursions.

We discussed it and we decided to wait until after Christmas, as it would give us time to think about and work out what he should buy. We had to get him the right bike this time as I didn't want to see him putting yet another in the box room to bury.

This wasn't as easy at first as it seemed. Stewart was kind of short and a kid's bike tended to look like a kid's bike, so without buying a girl's bike, we needed to find something his size.

We started the usual way of looking through the internet and our local bike shop but I told him not to bother there, not because they didn't have any good bikes but quite the opposite. They only had top quality good bikes for the serious rider, with a starting price tag of £400, and what he needed really was something he could use for a little shopping but mostly use for going out on fun rides with Mark and me. He was never going to spend a day cycling around the hills and woods of North Kent or riding off road on rutted flint trails, hopping over muddy ditches or anything like that. The bike had to be comfortable, didn't have to be fast so didn't need lots of gears but it did need a low ratio so it could get up the hill along Joy Lane.

That meant an upright bike was probably best, but most of the uprights around our way were aimed at women, with flowery baskets on the front and a space for a child seat on the back. The commuter or hybrid types, even the ones they sold at our bike shop, you needed to be my height or taller just to get on to it and if you couldn't put your feet down when you stopped, without leaning to a forty-five degree angle first, then they weren't safe to use on the road as he'd always be falling over into the path of the traffic, so we had to discount them from the list.

A mountain bike wasn't an option. He didn't want one, not after the last one, and to make sure he would get a good one, we were back into the £399.99 bracket, more than he could afford or wanted to spend on a bike that he was basically only going to ride along flat roads, the sea front and one long but ultimately gentle hill. If he had planned to ever ride to Canterbury on it, then having a mountain bike might have been an option. He would have needed one to ride the Crab and Winkle Way. But Herne Bay was the furthest he was aiming for and once he'd left Whitstable, it was all flat until he reached the other end.

He also didn't like using gears and, though an electric bike was out of his price range, we started to look at single-gear bikes, ones that could freewheel and had two brakes, which were becoming popular. There were even a few on the estate so we could see them in action. But I had reservations about them, even though Stewart seemed keen to have one. So we kept looking. But again, unless he wanted a girlie pink one, it was hard to find one in his size.

Then by chance we came across a cruiser bike. Admittedly the first one we saw was over £1000, fashioned in a gothic heavy-metal styling, but they had mass-produced ones too. Looking at them, some came with gears, some without, and it seemed the fewer gears you had, the dearer they became.

Then he saw the Ecosmo.

Unlike any other on the page, it came with a rack. Its handlebars were more up and straight back, in that Dutch style, and even had seven gears. It was affordable, not as cheap as the supermarket bike, but cheaper than the other cruisers, which from what we could see from the images were built just the same way, had the same fixings and style of mudguards and so on, but again it wasn't in that enthusiast price bracket either and half the price of the next cruiser with six gears which had no rack or reflector on its back mudguard.

Its height was at the maximum he could manage.

So, spring 2015 he bought it.

He loved it but for the seat, which was changed for one with more padding, and he rode it a couple of times to the bowling alley, but chiefly, for the first year, he rode it when we went out for rides together, during our bowling break.

However, Mark and I had much faster bikes and though we kept to a slow pace for him, I could tell he was getting disheartened that he wasn't keeping up. So, on one trip to the bowling alley, I tried his bike and yes, it was easy to ride and well balanced, so that winter, I decided to by myself a new bike.

I had two at this stage, his old mountain bike, which he had given to me when the new bike arrived, that I used to go to Herne Bay on as its tyres were better for bouncing over the concrete esplanade than my other bike, which too was showing its age. The dilemma was to either spend the next few years keeping it on the road or get rid of it. I decided to get rid of both and buy a new bike.

In fact, I was able to buy two for the price I would have spent on just one normally as I caught them at the right moment, in the sales. I bought a new hybrid I could use for fun and a cruiser, the very same as Stewart's, which I was going to use as my shopper.

When Stewart realised I'd brought a cruiser too, he was surprised, then delighted, and it rekindled his desire to get out and cycle more. I had felt he had been stressing that he was too slow and blaming himself for us taking so long to reach our destinations, but now he was wanting to ride whenever there was a good opportunity, something which thereafter never left him.

Initially it was only a trip into Whitstable, bowling or shopping, that we rode together and I was still somewhat quicker though that was more down to me trying to ride the cruiser like a hybrid. But soon I learnt how to ride in a more relaxed way, changed the saddle and found that the bike I was meant to be riding occasionally became my main bike and my 24-gear, lightweight, indigo sports hybrid was only really being used to do circuits, very early in the morning, a run out to Graveney, down Monks Hill, on to Dargate and back, or fun rides like a circuit to Canterbury, Herne Bay and home.

Now though, I had to get rid of the others and though I had considered just taking them to the dump, both were, with a little work, mechanically sound. So we decided to give them to charity, for Africa, giving bikes to people in poor, remote areas of that continent.

I thought the nearest drop-off point would be Halfords Herne Bay and asked Stewart if he would like to help me by riding the old mountain bike there. After all, he could never reach the floor on the old hybrid, even if I'd removed the saddle. He agreed but then I checked where to take the bikes on the website and discovered it was Margate.

He was a little terrified I was going to make him cycle all the way. But when I explained we'd cycle to Whitstable Railway station and then cycle from Margate station, the back way, with no traffic most of the way, he was fine, so that following week, we made the trip.

The distance to the railway station from our flats is 2.1 miles and traffic permitting, takes about ten minutes.

It was a wet day but only light drizzle. By the time we set off and we reached Whitstable Station just after ten, with no traffic to speak of, it had stopped and the sun was already poking through the clouds. I bought the tickets and we waited about ten minutes for the train.

We were lucky enough to find that there was hardly anyone in the last carriage, so bikes near the sliding doors, we took a seat nearby and I started to tell him a little about my history coming from there, letting him know he was going to see some of my old childhood haunts.

From Margate station, via Tivoli Park to Halfords is about 2.5 miles and takes 20 minutes, with two minutes, which felt like ten, to get across College Road to go up Nash Court Gardens.

He was nervous at first but relaxed enough to enjoy the trip and, after leaving Margate station, we rode up towards Tivoli Park, took the path behind Salmestone primary school and then followed Nash Court Gardens all the way through to Nash Court Road, not seeing a single moving car or person in all that time. It was now sunny and we just chatted as we reach the top of Nash Court Road.

I pointed out where my parents' old house was, although we didn't go down the hill to take a look and instead headed down the hill the other way and joined the Ramsgate Road. Now they've made some improvements there, dividing the pavement into a cycle lane on the opposite side for the road, so we crossed, then rode up the hill, and to his credit, even though I told him to push it, he rode up the hill as well.

What I had neglected to tell him was that Margate has two Halfords listed on the internet, one by the Hornby Museum and a big shiny one, just as you come onto the Westwood Cross estate. Both show up as Halfords on the Google map so I checked with the Charity's details but they just list it as Ramsgate Road, so that's both then.

But as we came level with the one by Hornby, it was clear it was going to be the other one, as it wasn't a Halfords anymore but a discount store. So we rode on, not too far as it happened, but at first it did seem it was going to be much further away, or I sort of thought it was much further, but then the last time I'd ridden this way I was ten, but at least it was cycle paths all the way.

We dropped the bikes off and once I'd signed them over, we left to catch a bus back to town. Only there was a Burger King by the bus stop and, in fairness, he had cycled hard to get that old piece of crap up the hill.

'Fancy a burger?' I asked, much to his surprise,

'Yeah, sure.'

The Burger King itself was a drive-through, so at that time of day, the restaurant part was quiet. It had been years since the last time we'd eaten in a Burger King year and so I treated him to a whopper, fries and coke. I had the same but with a tea and we sat calmly in a place where we outnumbered the staff and with no other customers and enjoyed our meal.

I made the suggestion then, as Dreamland was newly re-opened, we should take a look. We would have to go past it to catch our train back. He thought about it and said,

'Okay. But can we get some bird seed first?'

'Sure? Bound to be a pet shop in town somewhere.'

I guessed I knew where there had been one. It was just a matter whether it had survived from all those years ago.

The bus back to town took us up around the hospital before we arrived in Cecil Square and so we took a look around the town, starting up in the more rundown area, where he brought himself some pet things and some really nice earphones for his MP3. Then we strolled down the hill to look around the old harbour area, having a coffee in one of the trendy cafés, and walked past the old-style sweet shop but he didn't want to go in.

We headed back up the hill towards the main town as he suddenly decided he needed to draw out some more money, which at first I thought was a good sign that he was thinking of having a ride or something in the amusement park. However, heading towards Dreamland, halfway down Marine Terrace with the arcades in sight and the roar of the funfair in the air, he started to have an anxiety attack and couldn't continue. I noticed his breathing was becoming laboured again and suddenly he needed the toilet. So we headed back to the shopping, or rather I should say ghost-town, arcade,

'Let's go home,' he said as he reached where I was waiting for him.

'Sure you don't want to go on the scenic railway on the way? We have to pass Dreamland to get to the station.'

'No.' He wavered for a moment, as if he was wondering whether or not if he should ask me something and then added, 'Can we get the bus? Only, I don't want to go back on the train.'

'Okay,' I agreed. 'Buses are just over here.' I pointed under the archway towards Hawley Square.

It was now a nice, blazingly warm, sunny day by then. The park-like square surrounded by those tall town houses looked like an ideal place to go and have a sandwich. I even suggested we should go and get one but he didn't want to move from the bus stop.

There was a bus which would take us to Estuary View so we waited for that. Even though it would take three times as long as the train, a walk down the hill to home was fine by him, and so that's what we did.

Over two hours later, a little exhausted but the old bikes disposed of, we were home and he'd had an adventure. It seemed the experience had made him eager for more, gentle adventures.

13

Now we both had a 'Beastie Boy', his nickname for the cruiser bike, he enjoyed cycling more. As I'd learnt ride it more leisurely, to just cruise letting time roll by, riding for us both became much easier and somewhat enjoyable.

For me more so I'd say. Before then, I'd always been in a hurry, not to the point of racing between cars or anything like that, but to a point where I was always trying to get the bike up to its maximum speed and would get annoyed with the traffic if it slowed me down.

If Stewart would see me on my old hybrid in town, whilst he was shopping or waiting for a bus, he'd shout out,

'Swiftly.'

And we'd just have enough time to exchange a wave before I'd be gone.

Now however, I was gently rolling into town. Even the mobility scooters were overtaking me, but I just didn't care.

As the Verso ended up being used for circuits on my own and as the desire to just race it around even on those circuits diminished to a point where I would just give myself an hour to go and enjoy the North Kent countryside and to hell with the speed or timing, my relationship with that bike softened too as the 'Beastie Boy' had soon conditioned me to enjoying the journey and taking my time. Even if I was just popping down to Whitstable to go and buy something in town, it was all about listening to the birds, looking at the sea rolling onto the shore and I became a relaxed, gentle cyclist because of that bike. No matter which bike I was then on, in no hurry, smiling and finding that people were smiling back as being on a cruiser bike seemed to make pedestrians friendlier too.

The Lycra brigade rushing about didn't worry me anymore. Let them. I was enjoying the gentle ride and as a result, when riding with Stewart, he found it easier to keep up with me, to the point that, by the end of that summer, he was almost overtaking me at times.

We would occasionally take the bikes shopping together during that summer, a couple of times to the Tesco supermarket but mostly in to town and usually for bowling with a little bit of a shop before coming home as he was still shopping online.

But for most of that summer, on every second Friday, whether Mark was there with us or not, Stewart insisted, we would ride along the seafront towards Graveney.

We had three main destinations on that route.

The Sportsman was the preferred destination when with Mark and was 1.7 miles away. Sometimes if the weather was particularly nice and we hadn't made it before the pub closed for the afternoon, we'd carry on to Graveney church, which is 3 miles each way.

But when it was just the two of us, we always went to the beach area, where the homes by the sea meet the sea wall, a small triangle of beach overlooking the Isle of Sheppey, which we would call the picnic stop, 0.8 miles each way.

There we'd watch the waves for twenty minutes or so as we chatted before riding home and having dinner.

We still went bowling once a month, a trip of 2.4 miles each way, but not as nice as heading out Graveney way as the route to the bowling alley is all urban. There's a lot more traffic and, for most of the way back, it's an uphill journey and the cruiser is a heavy bike at 19kg.

When there were three of us, two on 'Beastie Boys', it was a long leisurely ride. If we could have swapped the cycle helmets for bandanas and, as none of us smoked, a candy cigarette or toffee cigars hanging from the jaw, then we'd have been sorted.

But the occasional drink at The Sportsman, a chat in their beer garden and a walk on the sea defences and a slow ride home was enough.

I'd discovered on one of my meanderings off the circuit route that there was another place, The Freewheel, 3.6 miles each way. He would have loved the place as it's a cafe as well as a pub, so there were treats to be had such as pies and cakes and a large garden out the back and is a haunt much frequented by the Lycra brigade so it wouldn't have mattered how old his jeans were or his sweatshirt, no one was going to be more ridiculously dressed than them. Unfortunately for 2016, I didn't discover the place until late summer, about early September, on what was to be my last circuit before the bad weather set in. That year it was quite a wet end to the cycling season, so we garaged our bikes from October to wait for the New Year.

We were planning to go at the end of that September, instead of a bowling trip. However, not long after I'd found the place, Mark became a carer for his mother and, though I was willing to go with Stew, just the two of us, when he had the enthusiasm for a long ride, the weather was very much against us and so we decided the three of us would go there, at least once, sometime the next year, during the summer break when the kids would all be at the bowling alley.

During that summer when the weather was nice, we would have a picnic by the beach. On a couple of occasions Mark was there too but normally it was just the two of us. We'd fill a rucksack with some sandwiches and crisps, take a can of beer each and spend half an hour looking out to the Swale National Nature Reserve at our picnic spot.

It was on one of those occasions that he mentioned that he used to fish around there.

Catching tench, bream, roach, rudd and perch. My only experience of fishing had been with the Cub Scouts along the Wantsum, catching eels, which was one of those fish he hated, but then he didn't like snakes either.

'So you like fishing?'

'Used to have my own rods.'

'Why don't you take it up again?'

'Could do,' he agreed.

He definitely gave it some thought.

'I don't mind coming but don't expect me to fish. I'll do some work on the computer.'

He smirked and after that day, he talked about fishing again more often. I think all he needed now was a few nudges in the right direction.

Because the road from our picnic spot was always quiet, even though it's narrow, we would ride side by side. He was happy even riding in front. It seemed the bikes were giving him a new lease of life and the confidence to take charge of things.

We would also ride on a couple of warm weekends during the summer, just the two of us, as far as the Seasalter Boat Club before heading back, just for the pleasure of riding. But on one trip there were a lot of the Lycra Brigade about, a devout group of people, who worship the road bike, ride about at fast speeds in gangs of ten or more, all with strange helmets with bird-bill points at the back and some with weird logos written on their bums who fly by, about an inch or two from your own bike, as they can't move out too far. Heaven forbid they'd lose the airflow, rhythm or speed or whatever the excuse is that they use to intimidate other bike users out of their way.

It was because of them we got ourselves some bike mirrors, as neither of us heard them coming so weren't aware of them, just enjoying the sunshine and the sounds of nature when they suddenly rushed by.

I've been cycling for eleven years daily, not counting my childhood years and those years had only been separated by my enforced years of car driving. Back then these people didn't exist but this time they even unnerved me, especially when one with Wanger written across both her bum cheeks in large white letters, or perhaps it should have been 'Wide Load' as she certainly didn't have the rear for Lycra, shouted something about having my saddle too low. She could talk. Her saddle could have fitted out a Rolls Royce and I'm sure she'd have been sacred in India.

Yet until the bad weather set in, he used that bike regularly and it was beginning to show as he was starting to lose weight and was constantly pulling his tracksuit trousers up, something he hadn't had to do before.

Then, on 23 February 2017, the best thing ever in the context of helping Stewart cycle more often happened and it was he who spotted it.

The opening of Aldi and Marks & Spencer on the Old Thanet Way.

As he received his benefits on Tuesday that week, we decided to visit and do our shopping there, to try the place out and if it was any good, we'd start to use it more often.

The distance to Aldi is 1.1 miles each way, so I said, as it was good weather, we should take the the the 'Beastie Boys'. It would be the first ride of the year and I reasoned that as it was a new shop and as we didn't know how much we'd want to buy there, it might not have anything he'd like after all and we could always shop for the rest online, so we could use the bikes to bring back whatever we bought and make the most of the good weather.

'Use the bikes?'

'Yes, we can fill our rucksacks and we've both got bungees so we could tie one of your bags for life onto the racks.'

'I don't know. It's a long way.'

'It's no further than our picnic spot,' I lied, knowing full well it was further, though not so much he'd really notice.

'But it's all up hill.'

'On the way it is, and anyway, you only have to cycle the Faversham Road bit and past the park. We don't have to go up Church Lane so we can avoid the traffic and you can walk it the rest of the way. I've already ridden the route once.' This was true. Once he'd told me that Aldi was opening a couple of weeks before, I'd taken my 'Beastie Boy' out to work out the best route, to make sure we could get over the bridge into the park area and I knew with those bikes neither of us was going to make it to the store without pushing at least part the way. 'And anyway, neither of us are against the clock. Does it matter if it takes half an hour or so to get up there? You haven't got to do it all in one go if you can't manage it.'

'But won't the bikes be heavy on the way back?'

'Yes, but we're going downhill virtually all the way home and what isn't down is flat. There's only one tricky part, the bridge we'd have to scoot the bikes round and that's only because they're too long to ride round the corner in one go. Trust me, I've been riding for years. It's not going to be a problem as long as you don't just keep buying stuff and remember we can only buy what we can bring back in a single load.'

He wavered and you could see he was thinking about it. Tongue running along the bottom lip, he was giving it some serious consideration.

'Look, there's an M&S food hall next door. They always have a café in a food hall.' Don't know if that's true but having already been up there, I knew there was one. 'If you ride, we'll have a cup of tea as a reward before we go to Aldi.'

'And a cake?'

'Only if you cycle.'

He thought about it for a second.

'Okay.'

We'd go early in the morning as it turned out both places opened at eight. We would get there by quarter past, adjusting our timing to eight thereafter when we realised we liked Aldi products and a quiet store suited Stewart as, after a couple of visits and the routine was settled, his anxiety reduced and the only heavy breathing he did was from the effort of getting to these stores.

I think he thought it would be a difficult ride but halfway, when the hill got steeper, and we'd get off and push. Even with the stops, we made it there quicker than if we'd gone into town. It took us about twenty to twenty-five minutes and the coming down was so undemanding that he was surprised just how easy the whole thing was.

So every shopping day, that's what we did. We rode up to Aldi, having a drink and a cake first at M&S.

By the end of February, he wanted to get a bike trailer as trying to get everything into bags and our rucksacks was making it an art to pack and balance the bikes safely and we were now having to use the kerbs to both get on and off the bikes once loaded up. This meant it was also a bit of a strain getting past the small bridge by the church, as we couldn't lean them because they were so heavy with the bags packed so full that there was a danger of tipping part of the load out into the stream.

He'd seen a trailer on a mountain bike on his way to get his pills and after looking them up online we found two types that could be fitted to the back wheel and were suitable for cruiser bikes, but I had a couple of reservations about both.

My first was that already with just a couple of bags he'd quickly got to the point of almost exceeding what we could carry as he could never stick to a list. He was always determined to spend his budget, so if the budget was say £60, that's what he had to spend. The concept of spending £40 and putting the other £20 over to something else, even after all the years of explaining it to him, he just couldn't do and it seemed he was always determined to fill all the space in the bags. One trip, we'd come back without using his rucksack, so the next week he'd bought even more to ensure that was filled too and we only just got it back.

A trailer presented a much larger space to fill. There was the chance his budget would increase so he could fill that space, that he might overload it and there'd be an accident. However, he needed something to keep the shopping from getting too high on the rack or else he couldn't have got on and off the bike safely, as even with the aid of a kerb, it was difficult to swing his short legs over the bag and, without buying another bike like a step-through, we had to reduce the height and take the shopping off the rack.

But my other worry was the overall length. He of course wanted the longest of the two trailers on offer and, without going up Church Lane and negotiating all that traffic, which would have been a nightmare had we been pushing those bikes with a trailer, the only real way up to Aldi was the way we were going unless we started a really long ride following the bus routes.

So the next trip, I took a draper's tape, having noted the width and length of the trailers including tow bar, and we measured it out against his bike in the alley and found we couldn't cross the bridge without unhitching first with either size of trailer as the bikes were too long, the alley was too narrow and there was no flexible joint where the tow bar met the bike or trailer. We needed more space than was available to swing round.

Would have been fine unloaded but the weight loaded would have made it difficult to re-attach. So it was back to the internet to find a better solution.

That's when we came up with the 'companions', actually pannier bags, but he always called them 'companion bags', one each side and easy to clip onto the rack. Although we loaded the bikes a whole Caesar salad too much on one occasion, on the whole, with them, the rucksacks and with a bag for life on my bike rack, we were able to buy more than enough food and things for a week, for less money than deliveries cost and after the first two weeks with the panniers, he noticed by the end of March how much easier it was getting going up the hill.

Once the panniers had arrived, we began to do two trips, getting something from the other two shops, all of which continued until after his birthday, only stopping because of a combination of severe bad weather and getting some beers in to watch the Women's Euros when we took a taxi. The extra drink wouldn't have fitted on the bikes anyway.

He liked his cruiser bike and along with the panniers, he started to express himself through it. He'd had the 'Ace of Spades' dust caps I bought him since Christmas 2015, but after I put some skull-and-crossbones caps on mine, this gave him the confidence to accessorise his cruiser bike, to customise it how he wanted it to look. Just a simple present, but now he felt he could do it. Those dust caps meant that he'd been given the seal of approval to do just that and so he did.

At first, I think he had been too conscious that people might stare or judge him for it, but that Christmas my parents had bought for me, I suppose concerned about a spate of stories in the press about cyclists being killed by motorists, a set of indicators that I could attach under the saddle and which worked off a button on the handlebars. I added them and suddenly the bike began to really look individual. They suited the bike nicely, even if they were a little redundant coming back from the shops with the bags obscuring them.

So when the new cycling season started in 2017, on that trip up to Aldi, he started to want to add things to his bike too.

At first he wanted some indicators but his saddle was so low there was no system that could be attached to the rack or saddle we could use. Everything it seemed had to be attached to the seat column, which he couldn't do, so instead, at Home Bargains he bought some more lights, using all of them at the same time, so you couldn't have said you couldn't see him as he had four sets front and back.

From Herbert's he bought a speedometer and when he bought the panniers, he also brought a pirate flag to fly off the rack.

By chance we also saw some handlebar indicators, the idea being that you tapped a button on the end and even those cars coming towards you would see the flash. We were planning to get them on 14 August as he had to get some new clothes first, something for the summer that would actually fit and not fall down all the time as constantly pulling his trousers up was beginning to get a bit annoying for him.

Going shopping now was a bit of fun, rather than a nightmare or a chore. We felt a bit like the dudes in Easy Rider. If I could have got a 'Stars and Stripes' cycling helmet, we could have imagined ourselves a sort of eco-friendly version.

His eagerness to get up there grew so much that he'd ring me the night before, after I'd just left, to remind me to be at his by seven so we could have a cup of tea before heading off. Then he'd ring me at half six, before he headed off to the Co-op to get his money, to remind me he was just getting his money so we could have a drink at M&S before we'd go shopping.

He was always in such a hurry to get going that we started getting there earlier and earlier, even before the stores had opened.

It was a good routine. First trip, park up, have a tea and cake at M&S, get pestered to hurry up, then shop, go home, unpack, tea, get pestered to finish tea more quickly, then off again, park up, this time have just a drink, get pestered to hurry up and drink it, then get a trolley and get a couple of items there such as a plant and a couple of dine-ins for two.

If Home Bargains was part of the equation, we'd shop in there first, then have the tea and shop in M&S. Seeing our two bikes, locked up side by side, his the lower-slung, dusty one, with its little flag fluttering, next to the taller saddle, shining paintwork and gleaming chrome one, it was like a pair of eco-friendly Hell's Angels had just breezed into town.

14

Of course, exercise alone wasn't the reason he was losing weight, getting fitter, healthier and livelier. There was also food.

Originally, in the early days I had just come round to be sociable and, seeing past the odd relapse, being around him was good company. In fact, after several months, another regular friend of mine was beginning to feel a bit stale and grating and by the end of the dark period was a friend no more. We'd drifted apart and then it ended. It made me much happier as, when I was visiting that friend, I'd be clock-watching to make sure I got back to Stewart's on time.

As Stewart's condition recessed, he'd physically showed he was happier in a smile, a joke, clowning around, little quips and wind-ups. He was beginning to express his feelings more, making me a cup of tea, something he hardly drank at this stage, but he'd make it for me, eventually getting to a point that every time he made a drink for himself, he'd end up making me one as well.

He'd initiate conversation and we'd talk about programmes we'd seen on the telly but it was food where we started to have our regular conversations, which in turn would lead to us eventually having more casual day-to-day conversations.

His diabetes and the arrival of internet shopping had made me more aware of what it was he was buying. The depression caused by the evil empire and its aftermath meant he had slipped into a junk-food diet and I realised if he was going to survive much longer, at least without losing a leg or something, then I was going to have to help him change what he ate.

Show him how to cook a healthy meal, or choose the healthy option, I mean, how hard could it be? Very, as it turned out, as people when they're in the depths of depression are like not real people any more, but it's as if they've been filled up with some kind of substance that makes them incapable of responding to anything. They don't hear, don't feel, and don't think. They're just, lost.

At first it seemed a hopeless task. I helped him cook a few weekday meals, making it with fresh produce from scratch but when it was his turn, he'd overdo things like the boiled potatoes, putting far too many on the plate, most of which would be thrown away.

He changed the plates for some designer brand with no proper rim, more like an extended flat bowl, filling them to the edge. I urged him to forget them, buy some new ones with a rim and they were never used again.

He brought himself a new dining set from the supermarket, a trendy square set, but again, in hindsight, a mistake as the trend of the day was for narrow rims and huge actual plate space.

Over the next year or two he got rid of them and bought another set of round ones with wide rims, his 'best plates', an old-fashioned willow-pattern set, which had a much wider rim than even the other more modern round plates and therefore a smaller plate area.

What shocked me was that even the modern round plate had twice the area of the old-fashioned style so, like most people then, without giving it a thought, I had been filling that flat area, thinking that was how much a meal portion should be and was probably eating twice the food I needed without piling it up on the plate and so, by 2015, with a much smaller plate area, the portion sizes fell.

It was little wonder the nation was getting fatter and the cheapness of our food was making it worse.

Before arrival of the 'Beastie Boys', he was getting more active, going to town more, but it was having no effect as he was now addicted to the crap food as much as he was addicted to sugar.

He used to have ready-made curries, priced less than £1, to cook in the microwave. I tasted one, horrid it was. I even joked that I doubted it was really beef in it, turned out it wasn't.

To try and get him interested in food, my first year's approach was to let him buy the meat for the dinners I'd cook for us both, that included Sundays.

It worked in part, getting him out and about. He'd buy the Sunday joint at Rooks, later to be named Paul's, and we'd get some mince with our online shopping. I would even write it out for him, like 'rack of lamb, French trimmed', but for almost a whole year, all we ate together was beef.

It didn't matter what I wrote. He'd either forget the list or forget he had the list on him or basically just say the first thing that came to mind which meant that one day when I had gone to all the trouble the day before to make some homemade mint sauce for the rack of lamb I was expecting, we ended up with beef.

A lovely joint but not the meal as planned.

It got so bad that first year, only buying beef mince as well, that our staple meals were chillis, bolognese, spag bols, cottage pies and lasagnes along with topside for Sunday dinners. I couldn't even get him to buy a chicken. If it wasn't for him wanting turkey at Christmas, I'm sure year two would have been the same.

By the end of 2011, the taxi fares to Tesco shot up by 45% overnight. Suddenly it was as dear as having a haircut, though they put their prices up a few months later by 35%. We moved to shopping on the internet and no more Tesco.

This helped his fight against diabetes.

When we had been going round the store, it was alright saying to him, buy this or buy that and have him buy those healthier items but the moment I bought anything for myself, he'd have the biscuits, the cakes, cheap apple pies and the fizz in the trolley before I'd found my Nori sheets. To make things worse, he'd take the trolley with him on his little rambles whilst my back was turned and so I wouldn't know the full extent of what he'd picked up until we were at the checkout.

It's always easier to find cheap apple pies than Nori sheets.

Even though he knew it was all junk, he still had to have it. He had cut down on sweets and sugary drinks but when in relapse, becoming less active and more withdrawn, he went back to the things that brought him more comfort and eased his pain, sweets, fizzy drinks, cakes and biscuits.

Lots of fruit and more healthy snacks like nuts and raisins were being thrown away and it seemed there was no way of helping him out of it unless you took total responsibility for him.

His carers, who were meant to do just that, went through a revolving door of staff during the dark times this time before they lost funding and vanished from the scene. But with the death of the Tesco trips and now shopping online at Asda, I at least had some control over what he could buy. He couldn't sneak extra things into the trolley, although he still had his sugary drinks. I suggested, and he agreed, mixing some of the bottles with the zero-sugar option and some of the ready meals were changed for Weight Watchers, low-fat yogurts and little things like that, and by the beginning of 2013 it was beginning to work.

But it wasn't enough. The shopping online and not filling the trolley on the sly meant to buy things like doughnuts, sweets and crisps he had to go to town to get them, so in a way, he was becoming more active and getting up earlier and getting out, even if it was still after ten, so he could get those things I wouldn't let him buy online.

He still had a plate-filling issue at this time; a healthy Weight Watchers quiche isn't all that healthy if you have seven or more boiled spuds and a 410g tin of beans.

This is why from 2011 onward we had started having a couple of weekday meals together as well as the weekends.

We started finding recipes from cookbooks, making the meals from scratch and not cheating such as buying any pre-prepared sauces. We started with simple traditional meals, chillies, pasta dishes, shepherd's pies, that sort of thing and saved the more spectacular for the weekend.

I used the books from my collection initially but as he began to like the whole home-made dinner experience, he would ask if we could have a particular one on a particular night. I started to expand the range of things to try, even to a point when we use to have a curry night.

He brought some books too, some from the charity shops and some of Jamie Oliver's latest series and Antony Worrall Thompson, but using them regularly was expensive, had little overall impact and quite a lot of it he didn't really like, preferring what I was coming up with from my older traditional books, so I decided to start collecting cuisine books from around the world to expand my repertoire but always sticking to the classics as it was working.

The result was now I was coming around earlier three days a week and the weekends to make him a dinner. He continued to cook for himself on the other days but he was still using the cheap and nasty ingredients, especially burgers and sausages, or ready meals.

It was a slow change, but as he began to eat a bit more healthily, he'd eat a bit more fruit, his reliance on cakes, biscuits and crisps dropped from being a daily staple to twice to three times a week and after 'the year of the beef', I was able to get him interested in fresh fish, something which over time became a more common sight on our menu.

Before 2010, we'd had big traditional Sunday fare, the most decadent being the three-course beef Wellington. Through the 'year of the beef', if it wasn't for my books and the nations of Germany, New Zealand and the United States, and the ways they do a joint, I'm not sure I could have kept the Sunday dinners interesting.

Doing things the same, but another way, meant the vegetables would change even if the joint didn't, and slowly things like honey-glazed parsnips, Yorkshire puddings and even on some occasions, roast potatoes were left off the plate and, by 2013, we were down to two courses with Yorkshires and honey-glazed parsnips an occasional luxury and, by 2014, they were off the menu forever.

By 2015, a beef joint was a rarity, with chicken and fish being the preferred staple.

During 2013, the Hairy Dieters book helped over the weekdays and it was good tasting food so unlike other diets, it didn't feel like we were missing out and being punished for being overweight. By 2014, it was clear he'd lost weight dramatically so now he'd hover between 42-44 and other people were commenting he had lost weight.

The only problem with the Hairy Dieters book, especially the really nice stuff like the leak lasagne, was that it took time and space to prepare, a whole kitchen in fact with all the preparation and yes, okay we had the time, but never the space.

A part of the condition is it made him withdrawn, want to shield himself from the world. That's why the curtains were never open in the bedroom and every windowsill ended up with plants on it.

It also meant, if there was a space sitting empty for a while, it wouldn't be too long before he'd buy something to fill it and spending half your time moving things to the floor or sifting through three canteens of cutlery looking for a potato peeler makes any recipe that takes more than twenty minutes to prepare feel like a chore.

Also, when you start making just the same eight meals in rotation over a week, food gets boring. Not everything in that book was as practical as a day-to-day meal but then in fairness in the book some of them were described as being occasional meals. You appreciate the meal, that's true, but you can't help getting tired of it and end up turning to the crisps, cakes and biscuits after the meal when watching television because they're more fun.

Alcohol again was something he didn't at first appreciate, thinking it was for Christmas or international football competitions and then drinking as much of the cheap stuff as possible. Never a big drinker, he'd started buying those three-litre bottles of cheap cider, to go with our meals, particularly for Sundays, so I introduced him to the joy of a good wine instead.

I'd buy a top quality yet affordable wine, buying it for its flavour not price or alcohol content and a glass and a half of that on a Sunday stopped him drinking the cider, so successfully, he ended up giving the old, dusty bottles away.

We even had a supplier delivering fifteen good bottles of Italian to us twice to three times a year and though we were having a bottle of wine a week, beer was only drunk at Christmas and during England football matches. By 2013, the only spirits we had were either to go in a meal, such as a flambé or rum baba, or for a cocktail on special theme nights on 'Strictly'.

15

He had become a well-educated drinker. He could even spot the difference between a good wine and some blended rubbish; even if at first he had trouble telling the difference by the label but, by 2014, if he bought a bottle to go with dinner on his own, he chose right. He knew what he was looking for on the label. He had developed a true palate.

When food was fun, he didn't eat any snacks whilst watching television.

He would still buy them and the bins were filled with unopened cake boxes, biscuits and so forth that had sat in the corner of the room and gone off. Now he was happier and so, to capitalize on his new-found adventures in food and willingness to lose weight, we started our first proper diet.

Starting from a point of already much healthier eating, now with less sugar in his diet, the next change wasn't going to be such a wrench. But I made a mistake. I treated the problem like I would have treated it if it was my problem, not taking into account that his condition would manifest itself from time to time for no apparent reason and on our first attempt, I came up with a diet that was a bit too extreme too quickly.

The idea was for three months over the summer of 2014, I'd cook a meal every day that would help him lose weight. I had a large collection of cookbooks by now and one, of wartime recipes, seemed ideal. We'd mimic the rules of rationing, using some of those recipes and also other recipes from other books, but still guided by that single principle of rationing. For example, we could save all our meat ration up for the Sunday joint and have fish to break the vegetarian diet during the week but if he wanted something with meat in during the week and still not use up the allotted ration, we would use Quorn as a replacement to still make chillies and a new recipe we'd found from America, a 'Sloppy Joe'.

Pork, in particular gammon, would also feature more, as you could have a bacon joint and chops or sausages, instead of a beef or lamb joint. I stuck faithfully to the recipes, including wartime recipes like Woolton pie.

We even rationed the sweets and cheese to what a wartime family would have had, although Stewart was allowed to have the whole ration and I kept those things at my flat so he wasn't tempted to go 'black market' when I went home.

He lost the weight, not quite getting below the magic number of under 42 which would have started the reverse of his diabetes, but his medication never got any stronger and after the Christmas indulgence, or England football competitions, he never reached the very big stage or had a double chin ever again, just always slightly over the reverse point, hovering between 42½ and 44.

He was certainly a lot fitter as he could even take a brisk walk to town and back, non-stop, which is an easy five-mile trip, without any problems. That first diet year, we would often go for a brisk walk to town and back on a Sunday afternoon, me doing most of the talking but he was definitely getting happier. There were fewer relapses, he started getting up earlier and, by 2015, he would often be up by seven at the latest, six to six-thirty regularly with a phone call to me after his breakfast to tell me he was up.

 He was impressed by the results at first, because they were dramatic, but as the body adjusts and the dieting gets harder as the gains reduce, I think he lost a bit of faith in himself and started to go out to town more on his own.

His confidence was certainly better and he remained fitter but he was sneaking off rations, having a burger puff with a fizzy drink. It was undermining the whole exercise and as the diet came to an end, I let him know I knew he'd been cheating. He didn't know at the time but I'd seen him at the bus stop eating a puff as I'd cycled by. I had suspected it for some time but I was coming back from booking a bowling trip a different way to usual because of some roadworks so I was on the road when he wouldn't have expected to see me and I'd come a route he wouldn't have expect me to use as it cut out the Horsebridge and Harbour Street areas of town, so really he was just unlucky.

In 2015 and 2016 we would do a summer diet again, in part to help get rid of the Christmas gains but also to help keep him generally fit and both those summer diets were aimed more to make him think about changing his lifestyle habits as much as they were about losing weight, as we indulged in more and more international dishes.

He carried on the effort into Christmas, if not completely. Instead of a whole turkey for him and his cat, he bought a turkey crown, not the smallest but one for three to four people, so he could have it over a couple of days and share some with the cat, which worked. The cat loved the turkey too and I could tell, as Jason put a little weight on over that time too. Even though he was always a slim cat after Christmas, he certainly had a bit of a bulge.

Stewart only drank beer when I was away. Though he had the wine, he never touched it until the New Year when I'd be back. He did overdo the sweet buying but, with his shrunken stomach and a new-found love of vegetables and being partly weaned off the sugar, I would come back after my fortnight away to find most the sweets were still there.

In 2016, I had to take a rucksack full of them, unopened, two boxes of luxury chocolates, six 500g packets of wrapped chocolates and six large bars as a present to the staff at the RSPCA in Tankerton and I still had a packet of each for myself. The diet plan was working; he didn't need the sugar so much anymore, even if the budget plan wasn't

That's not to say he still didn't have his regular fizz or his squash, but with the no-added sugar and mixing half the zero fizzy with the regular fizzy he was definitely taking on a whole lot less.

Saturdays and Sundays weren't so bad, as they were 'push the boat out days' where I would do something more challenging. We'd have something Cuban or a Moroccan Tagine or sea bass. We also started getting some different meats, from a company online, after a visit to Canterbury that previous Christmas we'd seen a stall selling ostrich burgers. We sought out a company online and so tried some ostrich, along with steaks, and other meats, such as kangaroo, wagyu beef, squirrel, rabbit, reindeer, zebra, partridge, a game-pie mix that included pigeon and even crocodile burgers, though wild boar sausages were probably his favourite along with kangaroo and, when Iceland started selling those two items from the same company, we stopped buying them online.

These things would make a Sunday dinner itself an event, not as they had originally started as a three-course banquet, of me showing off my culinary skills, but now, as windows onto the different flavours of the world, albeit with an eye on the calorie count, as no meal before the wine was added could be over 1500 calories all in with the main not exceeding 650, and as he only had toast for supper, even Sundays were healthier.

We hardly ever had a traditional roast again.

It could be anything from Belgium rabbit stew or kangaroo with spicy pickled onions and endive salad or with a Mexican salsa, enchiladas or sea bass stuffed with lemon and fennel.

The summer diet still had to have its set of rules. One day had to be fish, two days had to be vegetarian, we kept the Woolton pie from the previous diet, introduced an egg curry and one day he would have to cook for himself. It was a way for me to see if he was learning, making these lifestyle change or not.

As a treat, once a month I would do my own special invention of a curry, which owes little to India except for the spices really, but is heavy on vegetables, with chicken, though if you were vegetarian, it would be just as great without the chicken and you wouldn't need to add anything to replace it as really it's a veggie curry with added meat. We did a version with beef and lamb but chicken was his favourite.

In my very original version I'd used coconut block and I'd made it a couple of times back in 2008 and 2009. To make it healthier, I substituted that with fat-free Greek yogurt.

Getting away from poppadoms and having naans, with a bit of chutney, and his own balti dishes, naan plate and chutney bowl set made a curry night special, particularly as we would have it on a Saturday when he could have a beer with it too.

He stuck better to these diets but it was clear at the end of the run that he couldn't have stuck on it much longer as he'd start to get moody after ten weeks. He had more energy and was slimmer and I suspect in his mind he reasoned he didn't need to stay on it anymore as he was now healthier.

The giveaway was when he started buying packets of sugary jam doughnuts from Sainsbury's for us both to eat watching a movie and stockpiling sweets again by his seat. The fact he hardly ate any of the doughnuts and only had a sweet binge every now and then told me his lifestyle habits had changed, even if his need to buy these things hadn't.

His portion control was better but when he was cooking for himself without me to oversee what he was buying, he would keep visiting Iceland for cheap burgers, pasties and sausages, so he hadn't yet grasped the healthy eating rules completely even if now he'd have them with lots of peas, carrots and fewer boiled potatoes.

But that might have been more a symptom of his condition as he was always quick to fill the freezer but reluctant to go down more than a box depth when looking to take something from it for dinner

Which was why, in 2017, when we went thought the freezer to make room for M&S and Aldi supplies, we found bags of really ropy cuts of meat and ready-made meals from Iceland that were dated from when the store had first opened in town.

2015 had been the year of buying those willow-patterned, old-fashioned plates but also of the kitchen gadgets, the food mixer, hand blender, the tagine, coffee maker, the Assam teapot to name just a few, and us actually using them.

In that year, after every meal we shared together, he would, after washing-up, make a fresh pot of loose tea in the Assam teapot, bringing the milk in its own little jug and two proper teacups, with saucers, though after a few months, he started leaving the saucers behind, and we'd both have a nice cup of tea just to round off a nice meal.

So in 2016 rather than repeat the diet strategy again, as before, I'd keep the elements he liked best and prepared more meals with meat-free alternatives, so all our bolognaise, lasagnes, chillies, shepherd's pies, sloppy Joe's and basically anything mid-week which wasn't with fish was either an outright vegetarian dish or with the meat substitute.

When the diet officially ended, I continue cooking these meals, only occasionally cooking something at home but ensuring he had something like fish or a vegetable pie to have in the freezer so he maintained the healthier diet and so, as we talked about Christmas and the diet for next year, he was unintentionally continuing with his step-by-step lifestyle change and it worked as, by 2017, he was more accustomed to a healthy diet and sought out some of the healthier foods to go in his shopping trolley, such as fresh veg and prepared salads, but he never used any dressings, even if they were supplied in the packet.

By the winter of 2016, the old-style roasts were totally gone. If we did roast anything, it would be like a Moroccan-style chicken, stuffed with mixed fruit, beef would be a steak medallion with a blue cheese sauce and as he wasn't one for too much sauce, his calorie count remained below 650 for a Sunday main.

Homemade puddings were a must.

Steam puddings and crumbles, rather than pies, with rhubarb and apple being our favourites, along with a Dutch chocolate pudding which uses whipped cream and translates as Heavenly Mud, and a Scandinavian apple trifle, which was basically puree apple with caramelised croutons in between the two apple layers and a thick cream topping, much lighter than an English trifle and could be made more easily just for two so it didn't linger on into the following day.

Keeping the Woolton pie, we added more curries to the menu, and to compensate for the loss of the Sunday roast, we would have fish at least once a week and a takeaway night, from either our local chippie or Chinese.

The idea now was calorie count and portion size.

Slowly it worked as, when the takeaway night first started, we used to have the large portion but he could never finish it. In the end, I was on the small portion and he was having a child's portion. Even the familiar dishes at the Chinese he always ordered ended up only being half eaten with the rest reheated the next day for lunch.

He probably didn't see it, probably thinking the pills were holding his condition at bay better but eating less and becoming more active, he was becoming bubblier, more assertive and more jokey.

He was also becoming more considerate.

As his interest in food increased, he went from just lounging on the sofa, waiting for the meal, to suddenly standing in the doorway.

'Why don't you go in the other room?'

'Just come out to talk.' Or he'd say, 'Just come out to keep you company.' And from then on, whenever I was cooking, he'd join me in the kitchen.

His confidence grew.

'Can I help?' he asked.

'You could lay the table,' I'd reply. 'Knives and forks' if that was all we needed and he'd go and sort it out.

Soon he was helping with the prep. If we were making an apple crumble, he'd peel the apples whilst I made the mix, and he'd also get out the equipment as I asked for it and the ingredients. It was like I had an assistant.

He even used the gadgets on occasion when we were doing something a little more complicated but whipping cream he always left to me as he was worried he might go too far and spoil it. Any chopping with a knife I did except for potatoes, which he sometimes quartered to help me using a small paring knife. Only I used the large knives.

He started to buy unsliced bread, which he would slice to go with most meals, and it became his job to clear the top of freezer of all the cereal boxes, the teapot, tea caddy and other objects to the bedroom so I would have some space to prepare the meal and plate up, as the constant battle to find a worktop space, no matter how many times we de-cluttered, meant it was the only solution if we were to continue having home-cooked meals.

There was the odd pre-prepared thing in the freezer, vegetable pies mostly, and so we could still make things reasonably fresh on the one week in four he didn't get any benefits. We did use a bolognese sauce and cheese sauce for lasagnes from 2016 onward, though with all the other things we were making, we were lucky to get one of those a month.

In the end, he only really left me alone in the kitchen to plate up as there was nowhere for him to stand without getting in the way.

Bread becoming part of the dinner helped to fill him up and stop him wanting a biscuit or anything like that afterwards and was probably the main reason initially why he'd stopped eating the Sainsbury's doughnuts and even if we were making a Quorn mince lasagne, we'd have it with a salad. He now only had meat twice a week and take-away day was when he had anything deep fried as I didn't even make a Chinese anymore.

He didn't even put much weight on over Christmas. Strangely it was me who ended up being the porker in that I put on an inch after seeing my folks so as 2017 began, I was happy knowing that I'd changed his outlook with regard to his relationship with food.

He was eating genuine classic cuisine from places like France, Germany, Holland, Finland, Denmark, Spain, Greece, Morocco, Cuba, Jamaica, India, Canada and the USA. He even tried and liked couscous, something that would never have happened when I first suggested it back in 2006. Now he loved it.

Then as Aldi opened with an M&S next door, he had the chance with his better appreciation for food to keep to a lifestyle where the changes made could be maintained.

It meant, in 2017, no more diets. Instead of copying slavishly what was in classical recipe books or sticking to a diet regime's rules, now we were going to use what was available and apply what we had been doing, using those principles to create a healthy meal.

He could ride up there, which would help to keep him fit, and instead of taking a list, we would decide what type of dinners we wanted and find what we needed to make it there on the day, discussing it both the night before, on the ride up and whilst going round the shop. Going so early, with no one else about, we could take more time. However, that wasn't quite the case.

On the product side, we did buy and discuss what we were buying as we went about things. The only problem was he couldn't take his time. We were always haring round trying to be out again almost as soon as we'd arrived. We would always leave the M&S cafe at twenty minutes past eight and be round Aldi, through the checkout, packed, bikes loaded and home, mine first to unload my bike, then to his and unpacked by nine, then be off again by half past to do the M&S shop. Because Aldi turned out to be cheaper than expected, he would then go to Sainsbury's and buy not just the doughnuts, but more bread as well, to a point where he could have up to seven loaves for a week.

'Why did you buy the extra bread? There's only two of us and we'll be shopping again next week.'

'One's for you.'

'Okay, but that doesn't explain the other two.'

'Yeah, well, but!'

And that was that.

'But what?'

'I don't know.'

Buying three TV magazines, having five loaves of bread a week and a coffee table full of fruit made him feel safe. He had enough food and if he did relapse, he wouldn't have to go out again for a while. I could see that and although I did try to make him see he didn't need to worry about it, it was better in the end, to make my point, roll my eyes, and then use the extra bread in a Scandinavian trifle or a bread-and-butter pudding, Italian-style tuna bake or a rhubarb hat.

As the weeks went by and he got used to what we could put on the bikes, the load amount increased. What he couldn't spend on food, even he appreciated there was only so much he could eat in the end, he ended up spending on other things, such socks, another bike lock, a radio and a fish pan, things it seemed just to make sure he'd reach his budget target.

'Not another frying pan, you've got three.'

'It's a fish pan.'

'A fish pan.'

'For frying fish.'

'Cheeky git, I know what a fish pan's for. More surprised you're thinking about one.' 'Thought it be a good idea.'

'It is, yeah. That's a good buy.'

He was starting to think about how things were cooked, also buying an egg poacher up there too.

'You know that's an egg poacher, not a frying pan?'

'Yes.'

'Do you need it?'

'I want to try a poached egg. I've not had one before.'

'You only have to make a swirl in a pan.'

'I know, but I'm no good at doing things like that.'

'Okay, fair enough. Get the pan then.'

'Will you show me how to use it?'

'Sure.'

So we had salad with poached eggs later that week.

We started having smoked sausage with kale mash or the same sausage with hot lighting, a Dutch dish of potato and apple mashed together. We could make the same dinner different each time, replacing the smoked sausage for Bratwursts or black puddings. It was simple but worked.

I was still counting the calories but telling him he wasn't on a diet, realising I was never going to be able to convince him that he didn't always have to spend the same amount of money each week on food. M&S became a way at least of spreading the cost and the quality around.

Their dine-in-for-two offers and their £10 deals, with the occasional item on the reduced shelves, created the need for the two trips and slowly he ended up with a freezer full of top quality food, not a cheap burger or fish finger amongst them, the only 'junk' element being three cheese and onion quiches we kept in the freezer as he liked quiche with a salad sometimes.

All this and he was still losing weight, his waistline proving it.

The change in lifestyle, in particular the filling but smaller portions, such as one bratwurst instead of three with his kale mash, meant he could still sneak a sweet or a bag of crisps. As he thought he wasn't actually on a diet, that he wasn't having to adhere to a set of rules, he had become more relaxed about the food, eating more fruit and, though now he wasn't officially on a diet and he bought more cakes and biscuits, he hardly ate any. They just sat on a chair near to me gathering dust. Eating more complex sugars in the bread and healthy dinners was taking away his cravings for sweets.

During the week we would have a pudding but it wasn't anything full of calories like we'd have on a Sunday but instead punnets of fruit, strawberries and raspberries, often with fat-free yogurt or if we'd had a curry, we'd have a tin of peaches to finish off the zero-fat Greek yogurt.

He couldn't quite give up the two packets of crisps, but instead of that being every day, it was really only three times a week, and the Aldi packets were smaller than the market leaders, so he was even eating less of them.

From 2016's summer diet we'd followed a strict set mealtime which became known as 'Rachel's arse' as part of his resurgent cheeky nature and a little mocking at my expense.

Actually, what it meant was when I came round at 2-2:30 in the afternoon, after a cup of tea, we'd put on the Channel 4 catch up to watch Countdown and I wouldn't start making dinner until the first game started. As a formulaic show, that would always be with a long shot of Rachel Riley by the board waiting to pick the first letter, but Stewart would say,

'You only want to see Rachel's arse.'

'It's a nice arse.'

'You know she's a lesbian.'

'Doubt it. She's dating that dancer she was with on Strictly. You know, Pasha.'

'Yeah, right.'

'I can promise you she is.'

'Still a lesbian.' He'd grin.

'I'm still not starting dinner until the game starts.'

'Okay then.' He'd sigh.

So if he was hungry at say midday, he knew he could have a small snack or wait it out and even with a fridge full of sausage rolls, ham and bags of sweets, he'd wait it out and that's another reason why he started to lose the weight. A regular routine and his system expecting food at those regular times meant he didn't crave to eat so often and his body was starting to work with him.

His fitness was clearly growing as the lifestyle change gathered momentum.

With the exercise of cycling to Aldi, then M&S and back, the energy workout was making his system work for him again. That's probably why for the first three weeks he wanted a milky coffee and a thick rich slab of chocolate cake.

But on one Friday, around March or April, on a very hot day, we needed to go to Home Bargains to get the cat some Dreamies. He'd run out and had planned to get some from Sainsbury's on the way back from bowling but they'd put the price up so we decided to push our 'Beastie Boys' up Borstal Hill, and go there instead. It was hot and we were exhausted by the time we got there. So after, we went into M&S for a pot of tea and an Eccles cake.

He was surprised how good it was and from then on, that was what he had as a treat.

He liked routine and liked the security it brought.

It's why he always came via the back gate to see me for a cup of tea. Even when the back gate had to be kept locked and you would have expected him to take a shorter route, there he'd be, baseball cap on and hands pointing straight like a runner, walking round. He'd always glance up to my kitchen window and we'd wave to each other but always that same route.

It's why he would ring me first thing in the morning if he wanted to chat or wanted me to come round or he wanted to come round for a tea.

Aldi was also wonderful because it was so close that if the weather was good on a Friday we weren't seeing Mark, we could pop up early in the morning, buy some things for a picnic and have one at our spot all in the same day. Though Mark never joined us that year for another picnic, Stewart got to use his wicker basket on several occasions as we had our lunch there instead.

In fact, we had so much, our salad sandwiches were more like Lister's chicken kebab in Red Dwarf X. We also had some mini Scotch eggs, sausage rolls, a pork pie each and a bag of crisps and some cheese and onion quiche and after them the sandwiches. We brought half of what was left back home with us and he didn't eat again all evening. His appetite for different and better food had matured and he wasn't just filling up on junk anymore.

Aldi was also good for salad packs, so you didn't end up buying huge amounts to throw away. All the packs were for two or four, like the Caesar salad, and so getting him to eat two salads a week was easy, even if one had to be with a substitute lasagne.

It only changed, in the last three weeks of July into August, when we were watching the Women's Euros, partly because we had more beer, one with each half of each televised game, and because of the bad weather and the extra supplies. We'd gone by taxi each time so for the first time since those shops had opened, we hadn't ridden up there, though he was still livelier, cheekier, wittier and more confident, able to go and see Mark and our other friend Robert all on his own, something he couldn't do at all during 2010 to 2012, thanks to the evil empire.

Once we started cycling to the shops, the doughnuts he was buying in town only I was eating. Buying them was all part of the habit, like buying us both a sandwich when he'd been to the Co-op to get his money, a habit he couldn't seem to break, even though again, he never ate his and more often than not, I'd find it a few days later buried under a newspaper or his pills bag and say to him,

'You didn't eat your sandwich.'

'I know.'

'If you're not going to eat it, why buy it? You're only throwing them away.'

'I'll eat it next time.'

But he wouldn't.

So his bin grew ever fatter filling up with the leftover doughnuts, cakes, biscuits and the extra bread and fruit he'd buy to eat for midday or whilst watching TV but didn't because he was already full.

16

'The eyes believe themselves, the ears believe other people.'

*

When all you hear is negative, from the news, strangers talking, arguments from other flats and in your own head, you start to think the whole world is a nasty place, so why would you want to go out there?

Television at first was just a crutch, a link to the outside world he wasn't really a part of and not really something he truly enjoyed. He used to be a little obsessed with the evening news but when I started bringing movies round, his relationship with it changed.

Most the movies he had, other than horror, had been shoot 'em up movies, no plot just a lot of killing. So, from an early stage, I'd bring a film round, like a comedy or a drama. This awoke his interest in films but even when we joined the DVD mailing service and would chose ten films each to be on the list, his choices were pretty much in the same vein as his collection, only older horror like 'The Children of the Damned' or war films, the only difference with these were that they at least had a plot.

When the dark times hit, he lost interest in films again, becoming stuck watching the same old repeats of old 1970s comedies and magazine programmes, none of which he was really interested in.

Ironically, that was a time when he needed the television more as he became more withdrawn, even making silly excuses not to go and see our friends like Mark, so if I hadn't come round as I did, he wouldn't have had any human contact at all.

He hardly talked and he was almost like a living corpse.

But he was appreciative of my efforts. I know this as sometimes I was ten or so minutes late, a call from someone else as I was leaving or my dinner taking a bit longer than planned. I'd arrive, see the startled, almost tearful anxiety in those eyes as if he'd been terrified I wouldn't come round and he'd have that laboured breathing as if he'd just run a marathon.

It was during this time he gave me a key to let myself in with and it was during this time that I would often find him lying either still in bed at three o'clock, having not been up all day, or on his sofa, the television not even on, staring at a dead screen.

He didn't even have the radio on most of the time, just lying around, on his cushions with a sad pout on his face and arms folded, like Bela Lugosi, but tipped over to one side.

If it wasn't for the pets, he probably wouldn't have got up at all in the day and it was due to me reminding him about his birds that they ever got watered or fed.

During this period TV always began with the news. He wanted to know what was happening in the world, so the news would be first.

'Shall I put the TV on?'

'Okay.'

'Simpson's are on.'

'No, news.'

Now the news isn't about all that's going on in the world. It's about choice events that have happened that follow a particular agenda, usually that of the owners and usually to attract viewers, so it tends to focus on things like conflicts and natural disasters but always with a political bias, so an earthquake in Italy gets a couple of days or more coverage, even if only five or six die, and an earthquake in Russia might get a glib mention but only if enough people die. Then it's down to their substandard, Soviet-era buildings rather than the fact the world just parted beneath their feet.

But if you're frightened and all you see is the world killing itself, is it any wonder you want to hide away indoors all the time? Then all the shows that follow on from there don't help.

You either have soaps, which now tend to be doom and gloom with less focus on the comedy, so unless you're into them, they're not the sort of thing you can drop into as and when without them making you feel like slitting your wrists.

Then there's the magazine programmes or consumer programmes, so you see stories about fake watches flooding the UK or uncapped immigration or you're watching some fluffy programme where two likeable people tell you about the night Elvis stretched his legs at Glasgow airport or why, in fashion, blue's the new green or whatever.

There used to be a time when there was escapism on the TV before the watershed and without it he would have to sit up until past the watershed to be entertained by something like New Tricks. But after all that fluff there seemed to be nothing but violent drama. Any true escapism didn't arrive until the weekend.

There were other shows but they tended to be food related and until the Hairy Dieters appeared, it was all rich and fattening food or baking cakes, that sort of thing, and often difficult to make, especially when your confidence is low, and were the sort of thing to drive him to nine rich teas and two bags of crisps per episode.

But as we started spending more time together, cooking, heading out bowling and so on, he became open to alternative suggestions and as I began to come round earlier, he began to open up again and find fun in discovering new things.

It didn't happen overnight but, in short, we ditched the fluff and the consumer programmes, the cookery book shows and the mundane late afternoon games shows where even a lump of chewing gum has a chance of winning the main prize, and headed towards the more intellectual, the factual, the comic, the light-hearted and competitions where the contestants were either like us or where they were all equally good but there was no attempt at any time in either case to ridicule or include people without any talent whatsoever just to be abused for a baying audience's pleasure.

As Saturdays became the worst for pointless crap, I suggested we'd make them a DVD night and started to use my own collection to bring him out of the doldrums.

His face started to show signs of joy, bright smiles and he'd even start making comments about films like Ghostbusters, The Pink Panthers with Peter Sellers, and Laurel and Hardy to mention a few. He particularly enjoyed The Blues Brothers, The Rocky Horror Picture Show, Tremors, Blade Runner and the anime Perfect Blue, a tale with at its centre the themes of paranoia, mental breakdown and murder. We also watched other films where the lead characters suffer from mental illness, such as 'Black Swan', 'Breaking Glass' and 'Time Square', all of which he enjoyed, I suppose because the heroes of the stories had the same condition as he did and weren't portrayed as some psycho killer but as real people struggling to overcome their disabilities and, more importantly, not letting their condition get in the way.

He even started to sit up more and a good indication as to whether he enjoyed something or not was how upright he was, the more interesting the more upright, though with a slight lean towards the sweets pile. Bored to tears and he was lying horizontal so then you knew it was either time to find a new show and, as I took control of the remote, we'd often have a little flick around to find something more interesting.

We enjoyed comedies, like Red Dwarf and Father Ted, and if when flicking round I stopped on something, he now had the courage to say,

'I don't like that.'

'Want me to find something else?'

'Yes.'

I'd listen to his opinion, even if it was just a simple sentence, such as his defining critique on the Blues Brothers.

'I liked the way all the cars crashed at the end.'

He became less worried about trying out new shows and if he didn't like it, he could say so and we wouldn't watch it all the way through or ever again.

I got him to watch documentaries on science and history subjects I most enjoyed and soon we were also finding things I wouldn't have thought of to add to that list of interest, such as 'Strictly Come Dancing', 'The Great British Bake Off' and 'Women's Football'. He liked 'Atlantis' and was very upset when the series was cancelled without a conclusion and got into 'Poldark', which he would never have watched before knowing me.

We began to experiment with different types of film genres, more so than we had done when renting the films, as he began to have a zeal for anything that was a little weird, even art-house, foreign films like 'Insomnia' and 'The Girl with the Dragon Tattoo' series, dubbed versions of course as he had trouble reading the subtitles fast enough to keep up with the flow of the film, which I discovered when we watched 'Betty Blue.

We watched anime and cult classics, such as 'Casablanca', 'North By North West', 'Bullit', 'The Third Man', 'The Lady Killers', 'Dr Strangelove', 'The Breakfast Club', 'The Italian Job', 'Some Like It Hot' and 'Rear Window'.

Comedies with Leslie Neilson, Will Hay and our favourites, Laurel and Hardy, especially their features, 'Sons of the Desert' and 'Way Out West'. He loved their slapstick humour and their magic together.

Regaining his confidence, and being mainly in recession, he became less withdrawn. All the satellite or broadband channels were gone by 2013. He was a Freeview viewer only and we started finding programmes he would never have considered before, giving him a new lease in life.

The return of Red Dwarf on Dave, with the promise of all those brand-new episodes gave him something to look forward to. He even talked about how much fun it would be to see the gang all back together again. We crossed our fingers the series would be good and it was better than expected.

As a result, he got into other shows he'd not tried before, like QI, finding it both funny and fascinating, and sometimes we would talk about some of the topics afterwards. This in turn brought about his interest in history programmes from repeats of Time Team to then new shows mainly on BBC2 and BBC4 as well as the science series with Brian Cox.

The Japanese version of Ninja Warrior along with the old Crystal Maze and Fort Boyard proved to be more entertaining than I even remembered. It was more fun to see people who, even if they had really good jobs you needed a university degree for, struggle to work out how to put a set of cogs on a wall to wind a candle under a string to release the crystal, which helped his confidence I'm sure, as it proved to him anyone could get even the simplest of things wrong at any time.

Thanks, Richard O'Brien for that. Had you not made the show so interesting and made it a hit, Stewart's recovery would have taken a lot longer.

Old episodes of Top of The Pops reminded him of happier times as they'd reached our teen years and seeing acts we had liked back then gave us things to talk about as we reminisced about those days.

We could talk about new shows we discovered, which no one else seemed to be watching, making them special to us, like 'Miss Fisher's Murder Mysteries', a must watch once a week. When that finished, we had the 'Avengers' to replace it, which for both of us became a real treat when they started to show the surviving episodes from the original Ian Hendry through to the Honor Blackman days, which were even older than us, but we were seeing them for the first ever time. They might have been old but were still the most original thing on TV pre-watershed.

And that was the problem with TV generally. If you have depression or any serious mental issue, you need something fun to entertain you, not things that keep enforcing how bad life really is, or show you things like new homes and cookery programmes about things you can't aspire to and you'll never achieve, which make you feel all the more worthless. We'd broken that cycle and it all started because of four dudes roaming around space in a large red mining ship, three million years from earth, and another pair of dudes in bowler hats, from over eighty years ago, who wanted to go to the convention by pretending to their wives they were going to Hawaii.

By 2014 it became rare to see him have a withdrawn day. He would get up early, go to bed regularly at half ten, only staying up late on a Saturday for Match of the Day and like myself having a lie-in on a Sunday morning.

Now he had things to chat about to other people and could actually have a conversation.

Originally he'd phone his parents and the conversation would be,

'How are you? .... Alright ..... Bye.'

When we started watching things like 'Strictly Come Dancing', the short-lived series 'Atlantis', 'The Great British Bake Off', 'The Factory' and so on, he'd ring either his mum or Mark and it would go like,

'Did you see Bake Off last night?.... Good, wasn't it?.... I liked it when that girl made that pub out of gingerbread..... Good, wasn't it?..... His was good too, but a bit over the top.... Yeah, going to watch Strictly?..... Okay, mother, I'll let you go. We're having shepherd's pie tonight.... Bye.'

Sometimes he was so eager to tell you about a programme or something that was going to come on, that the first sentence was rushed and so fast, you had to ask him to say it again.

'Don'tforgetthenewRedDwarfstartstonight.'

'What? Slow down.'

'Don't forget the new Red Dwarf starts tonight.'

'That's right. I know. We saw the trailer last week.'

'It's going to be good, isn't it?'

'Should be. They've never made a bad episode yet.'

'No.'

'Okay then?'

'Yeah, okay. I'll let you go. Don't forget tonight.'

'I won't.'

'Bye.'

'Bye.'

Then, as he became more and more excited about something, his voice got louder to a point that sometimes, in the kitchen, he come in and,

'They're at a baked bean factory tonight.'

'Don't shout. I'm only a yard away. You're hurting my ears.'

'Sorry.'

'That's better, indoor voice.'

'They're at a baked bean factory tonight.'

'Who are?'

'The Factory.'

'Oh, yeah, great. Should be interesting'

'Yeah.'

To make some of the shows more of an event and therefore more entertaining, we started to build a food theme night around them. Football was easy. That was just a matter of a beer each half and during the World Cup competitions, when there was more than one game in a day to watch, we'd have some easy food to go with it, such as pizza, salad or a homemade curry.

But we began to translate this into other programmes too. 'Strictly' had its theme nights so we decided to have a theme night too. On Hollywood night we'd have an American-themed dinner, which could be anything from 'Sloppy Joes' with fries or hotdogs with some left-over Quorn chilli smothered over the top or a steak with sweet-potato mash. At Halloween we had something like a home-made curry and, with the Blackpool Tower Ballroom night, we'd have fish and chips, but all three came with a home-made cocktail, usually a screwdriver or two, and it became a set treat, a regular event in our calendar.

Having a new-found love for history and science meant he enjoyed historical set dramas, as well as documentaries about the Tudors, the Wars of the Roses and the like. He now demanded to be entertained by what he was watching, becoming frustrated by slow, ponderous, pointlessly dull dramas and wouldn't give them a second episode. He had gone from lying facing the box, accepting whatever, to finding what he enjoyed. He was asserting himself and it was keeping the demons in his head at bay.

With his new-found interest in different film genres, when he would pop into Sainsbury's, on his own primarily, despite my protests, and buy a packet of five jam doughnuts, if there was anything new that caught his eye, a DVD or a CD, he bought it.

His action movies were now more comic, like 'The Expendables', or anything with Jason Statham, to 'The Fast and The Furious' series and the Marvel and DC comic book series. He didn't buy any horror movies anymore. In fact, he didn't even watch the hundreds he had, so many of the older DVDs sat in the corner, to a point where they became coated in a thick layer of dust and it wasn't just because they'd become part of the fortifications. Often when we were looking for a movie to watch, I'd glance over to one and suggest it, and he'd want to watch something else instead.

It even got to a point at times when he was making the suggestion as to which movie we should watch and it was me dithering as to whether I wanted to watch it or not.

The nearest he got to horror again, from 2014 onwards, were the comic parody or the old B-movie sci-fis, such as 'Them'.

By sheer chance he bought from a charity shop the complete set of 'Tremors' films but had hidden them under the coffee table along with a lot of boring films, some of which we'd watched and about halfway through knew we'd never watch them again, no matter where in the multiverse we'd be, and they'd sat there for a couple of years until early 2017, when on a Saturday wondering if we should watch a repeat of a Miss Marple we'd seen too many times before or watch a DVD, he said to me,

'Let's watch a DVD. You choose.'

So, for a change, I looked under the coffee table and noticed the first film in the 'Tremors' series. Now I'd seen the first two and knew they were good, fun entertainment so I suggested we try them.

He was a bit sceptical at first but willing to try and, as it turned out, for the next five Saturdays, we had a fun movie to watch after dinner, taking us through the lean two hours before Match of the Day.

His attention span was also increasing as he could sit through, without either losing the thread or getting bored, epic modern movies like 'King Kong', the entire 'Lord of the Rings' and 'Hobbit' trilogies, even if he did question why the Hobbit films were so long for such a slim story. I'm not sure he ever got the concept of film directors' egos and studios throwing shed loads of cash at them to feed them.

He was even getting critical of Bond and pointing out plot holes or contrived sequences such as with the DB10 as contrived.

The nice thing was, he was finding, that if he made a comment like that or expressed joy about a film, like with 'Tremors', he was genuinely disappointed when the franchise came to an end. But now we could talk about any scene in the film openly and often that would lead to a more in-depth discussion about the film as we'd carry on talking about it over the TV programme that was on while we waited for the football. In the end we weren't being bored by that and the evenings were ending on an emotional high.

As a result, his moods were often light and happy, and a relapse now looked more like a moment of deep, thoughtful contemplation rather than a total withdrawal from life and existence.

He was watching the news less but now buying regularly a newspaper, virtually every day, although, going by the leaflet litter inside, he seldom read them, at least before I had, and for some reason, three TV guides a week.

I used to say,

'Why three magazines?'

'I don't know.'

'Why not just this one?'
Pointing to another one he'd say,
'I like that one.'
'Then buy that one then.'
'But we can have one each.'
'Okay, I get that, but there's only two of us. Who are you buying the other one for? The cat?'
'Don't be silly,' he'd grin and say, 'I know.'
Then one day, he brought just one.
'I don't believe it. Just one TV mag.'
'I know. I really tried not to buy the others.'
'Good for you. I'm proud, mate. Good.'
The next day, with the paper he'd bought the other two.
'Why did you buy the other magazines?
He grinned and shrugged.
'I know. I can't help it.'
At times, he would get excited about something and struggle for the words, finding it very difficult to express himself, even to a point when he would get annoyed with himself, so TV became a way of channelling that expression. If he liked an artist on Top of the Pops and wondered if I liked it too, he'd say,
'That was good, wasn't it?'
Always 'wasn't it?' as if he needed to know if I approved too and then it must be good.

Sometimes a programme would warrant some comment afterwards, such as a programme we watched about the many ways death is celebrated around the world and the ways of disposal, and that led us to a discussion about how we'd like to be disposed of, but not in the morbid way he had talked in those dark days, but as in celebration.

A programme on string theory led to a two-part conversation that continued on one of our rides up to Aldi. He was wondering what an alternative version of us would be up to and whether they'd be riding up to Aldi to get their quiche and salad too.

Maybe not a discussion on the same metaphysical level as the show had been about, but it had made an impact and had opened his mind to other possibilities, as he liked the idea of an alternate us. He learnt what colour was and discovered various other science subjects but without it becoming or feeling as if he had to learn. This was fun, not school, and there was no test at the end of it so he wasn't under pressure to remember it all.

The return of the Crystal Maze, with their Celebrity Special, proved to be good but in a different way to the originals and, although we knew the celebrities on the whole were only on it to promote themselves, he was really eagerly awaiting the normal people's version later in the year, already planning that we should have a beer with it and make it our new curry night.

Drifting away from the news, he got into the Simpsons and with a new smart TV he bought in March 2017, through the magic of YouTube we didn't have to watch the news at all anymore. In fact I only kept up with world events now via those newspapers and the radio during the day. Instead we found a light-hearted action series, 'C.A.T.S. Eyes', and 'The A-Team' being repeated from the first episode on a minor channel made the early evenings fun.

The trick to help keep the depression away and maintain a happy frame of mind was through storytelling and fun entertainment and it was working as I knew it would. Media influences our outlook. If it didn't, then most toys wouldn't get shifted at Christmas. In fact the more lively the product and yet the more logical the plot, even if the manner in which they achieved it wasn't, was what kept the demons at bay. A show like C.A.T.S. Eyes had defined goodies and baddies and the A-Team was just pure escapist fun and by cutting out all the shows that promoted alcoholism, that is to say, the leads seemed to have a glass of wine at any given opportunity like the characters in the fifties used to have a cigarette, and avoiding shows with cruel malice and violence for 'drama's sake', we were making the world a fun place to be.

So, from the end of March, along with our eating changes and riding up to Aldi every week, we had developed a new routine for every weekday mealtime. We'd start getting dinner with Countdown, then 15 to One until that finished, when instead we watched Scooby Doo. After Stew had washed up, C.A.T.S. Eyes, The A-Team, The Simpsons on catch-up, then either a comedy on Dave or Top of the Pops on BBC4, then The Avengers.

No blood-splattered deaths, arguments, glasses smashed against the wall in frustration, lush activity, malice, backstabbing, snide behaviour or adultery amongst any of them, just a lot of laughs.

He became more lucid and was enjoying life more. Other people had noticed how much friendlier and how more communicative he was, that he would talk to them at the bus stop or if they saw him sitting out front, something he'd never done in the first eight years he'd lived there.

He was enjoying life so much now, he didn't even notice when he was eating two healthy salads a week, without dressings, and meat only once a week. The effects were showing. His stamina was up and he was getting to sleep and sleeping more regular hours. He wasn't feeling tired in the morning or lying in bed worrying all night.

Sport was still a big factor but, instead of sport for sport's sake, it had been cut down really to just football.

The Premier League was one thing, England's men and the international competitions, was another. Thank God for the Welsh as at least they gave us some pride in the last men's European Championships. But something which suggested one boring weekend ended up being the most enjoyable football outside the closing fixtures of the Premier League season.

England's Women.

We'd caught the Euros first and the football itself had been good, without all the rolling around and diving theatrics and, although the England women had done as badly as the men that year, they changed the manager and so now under Mark Sampson we gave the Women's World Cup a go.

If only the men had as much heart and if only Lucy Bronze was named gold, as we won bronze by beating the Germans.

So come the Europeans in 2017, he was ringing Mark and his parents, telling them to watch the England games. We had the beers in and watched every game we could get on regular TV, as Channel 4, for all their advertising, didn't do the sport the justice they should have done, especially compared to the Paralympics and F1, where they even now televise the practice laps. Not even Murray Walker would have gone that far. We delighted in beating the French and felt unlucky to go out to the tournaments eventual winners, Holland.

It was like watching the Welsh men all over again. But even in defeat, we were still filled with pride for the Lionesses, the English ones, not the Dutch, who were also called the Lionesses confusingly enough.

17

Schizophrenia is an insidious disease as it robs people of their personality, by making the victim paranoid, withdrawn and anxious all the time. People who know nothing about anything just dismiss this as being crazy or them as being lazy but, to get by, routine and habits form, created by the sufferer to bring comfort and easy of mind.

The house was one of those comfort areas that eventually got a bit out of hand. The space filling and the fortress building was one thing but it also meant he struggled to leave the fortress for too long, particularly when he was already stressed. It was one thing going out and becoming anxious as the adventure wore on but particularly in the dark times or when he was having a relapse, he was anxious to such a frenzy that the very idea of stepping outside the door was enough to put him into a panic, even if he was just taking rubbish to the bins, and this happened quite often on a Sunday, particularly before we got into the happier television routines from 2014 onwards.

In those first five years, he had a couple of neighbours who we used to see and visit very occasionally, but he never liked staying at their flats too long. Initially I didn't understand the need to get away all the time. Okay, one of them, Angela was a bit scatty.

She even made us a Sunday dinner once, which was more fun for being such a disaster than either cultural or edible. If only the cider had been drinkable, maybe it wouldn't have seemed so bad and we might have done it again.

However, it was on such occasions that his anxious breathing would begin just as we were heading back to his place and, despite the comedy of errors of Angela's afternoon, it was soon obvious he only felt relaxed and calm in his own place.

The one or two neighbours who came round were more fair-weather friends, either coming round to only watch the football and have a free drink or to come round and whine on about their ex, their children or whatever else they could think to whine about but, by 2011, even they had fallen away and there was really just the two of us.

Through the dark period all these people had abandoned him so as he began to recover and improve on his old self, as these people never came back, reduced to only a wave or 'Hiya' in passing, and as his confidence to be himself and keep these people at bay improved, he never invited them or accepted any invite from them again.

He became more relaxed and comfortable spending more than just a few minutes at my place, one of the few places away from home he was happy to spend time at.

On a few occasions fate would ensure we were there for a good evening as one time, his cooker died and we had to have Sunday dinner at mine, and another when I had to wait in for a parcel so we brought everything over to mine and had another Sunday dinner there, but on the whole, he would want to get back to his place as soon as he could, or after a couple of cups of tea and a little chat.

Just couldn't settle outside of his own flat.

In the first five years, when I was still making my own dinners, he'd patiently wait, watch a DVD whilst I was busy in the kitchen and badger me to hurry up with the washing up so we could get back to his by five.

After the dark period, as we started having Christmas drinks and bowling, the time span lengthened, as seven thirty became the new five, but it always took the same pattern. After a while, whatever we were doing, even if we were all sitting around the table with our hot chocolates after bowling, he'd quickly drink his, rushing it almost, then start looking at his watch or the clock on the wall.

'Shall we go now?' he'd ask.

At a neighbour's that was easy. At the bowling alley, finishing the game at three with the next bus back at four thirty, his tack would be to add,

'Come on. We need to go shopping.'

'What for?'

'Sunday dinner stuff. Milk. Paper.'

'Okay. Let me finish my drink then we'll head off.'

'Well, finish it then.'

'Okay, in a mo.'

Then when we'd leave, he'd be briskly walking into town, getting the two or three items which couldn't wait until Saturday, and then home.

As his flat developed, and the DVD walls began to be built, his home became a place he genuinely began to feel at ease in.

The soft toys up on the ramparts, all along the backs of the two sofas and on top of the DVDs on the shelves, were like his lookouts. The plants on the windowsills, with varying degrees of longevity as he wasn't one to water them often enough, became more of a screen so other people couldn't see in as, now the depression was abated, he now didn't like closing his curtains.

He did try to look after them. He even bought himself a small watering can to make leaning over the DVD barrier between window and seat easier, only like the herbs in the kitchen, he struggled to understand that sometimes plants need watering more than once in a week and sometimes, like the herbs in summer, need watering twice a day.

As time passed and he filled the spaces, he relaxed more, but it became harder to keep the place clean, as by then he only cleaned the areas easy to get to. Places hidden by the ramparts, he didn't care about.

One Christmas before I returned from Wales, he decided to take all the decorations down but as he couldn't reach the pins and wasn't very good at balancing on the arm of the sofa, he just pulled at the chains and brought them down that way. For the next three years, up in the ceiling the pins remained, making it easy to know where to put the decorations each time, but each time he did this, for the rest of the year there would be little tufts of decoration hanging on the ceiling as if there had been an explosion in a tinsel factory.

He had lots of pictures on the walls, from dragons to aircraft, boats and surrealist art, which, until he ran out of wall space, he kept adding to but always in pride of place was a set of pictures of his cousins, Anthony and Connor, both of whom he was proud of and he would often keep me updated as to what was happening in their lives.

He had two televisions in the bedroom as well as the one in the lounge, all which had to be connected up to DVD players. The set in the living room, through a channel box, was connected up to eleven different players, mostly DVD, but also a Blu-ray, a games console and two VHS machines, mostly bought from the charity shops, and so behind the television resembled the inside of a telephone exchange with Scart leads everywhere and that of course didn't include the TV's built-in DVD player.

Again, they were a security blanket. If a DVD jumped or didn't want to play in one machine, it would in another but, as 2017 began, he seemed much more at ease, putting most of the players, but for two, along with the Blu-ray and the console, into storage in his box room, along with his four full-to-bursting tool-kit bags, his electric drill and the Christmas tree.

Because he always had to be home as soon as possible, it meant that some things he wanted us to do didn't happen.

As his confidence and sense of adventure grew, he started to make plans for things to do in weeks or months to come. He wanted to go to an Indian restaurant but as they didn't open until seven, it didn't happen.

Then there was the new gastro pub and as Whitstable became more 'hipster', more new restaurants opened. It began to feel like almost one every month, all I know he would have liked to have tried, but as few of these places opened around two to three in the afternoon on a weekday, he just couldn't. Even with the promise of going each way by taxi wasn't enough to have him venture out after seven and he wouldn't do Whitstable on the weekend because of the crowds.

Even our Christmas meal happened after bowling at about half three at The Peter Cushing and by six he'd be reminding us both that we ought to be leaving soon to get the bus.

As a result, we couldn't go and see a pantomime or go to the cinema other than if they had an afternoon showing and then he would only want to go to the one in Herne Bay. He didn't like the crowds in Canterbury as that city became more student orientated.

He did like to visit the town during the day, often taking the early bus so he could visit the charity shops and get his pills. After the dark times, his confidence and his energy growing as we started to change his lifestyle, he'd spend more and more days down there, until in the last three years, during the good weather, he'd be down there every weekday, sometimes not even to buy anything, just going down, looking around the shops, having a drink whilst waiting for the bus home again. Often he'd go early and be back by half ten, only to go out again around two as his pills weren't ready and I'd get a phone call.

'Can you put the kettle on?'

'Where are you?'

'Waiting for the bus.'

'So you're in Harbour Street?'

'Yes.'

'Okay, I'll put the kettle on in ten minutes.'

'Okay. Bye.'

Then I'd go round to his place and by the time the kettle was boiled, the bus would arrive and he'd come crashing into the flat, breathing heavily, but with a grin on his face like a child who'd just got away with doing something they shouldn't have.

In the early days, he did drink a lot, almost some kind of drink every hour and after the dark period, he was almost obsessed with making me a drink each time too. I'd gone from having to make myself one all the time to hardly having to when at his but as he got fitter and healthier and less dependent upon sugary drinks, he started to drink less frequently and we could even go out for half a day and not have to have a drink so often.

When we took the bikes up to Halfords, he'd had three drinks over the course of the whole adventure, though he made up for it when we got home. To some degree, in the later years, it became more of a routine to make a drink, including a tea for me, to avoid the adverts or before something we enjoyed came on, so we wouldn't need to get up at any point and miss any of it.

From 2013-17, he was out there, living a life, but always eager to get back home and the comfort of his surroundings by no later than seven.

We did on occasion go further afield, to Herne Bay to see Mark for a coffee. Sometimes we rode but often we went by bus. In the summer with all the people along the beach, it might have been too daunting for him, even if going to The Sportsman was as far as going to Herne Bay though, by 2017, he was coming round to the idea of us both on our 'Beastie Boys' taking a ride over there, but after the school summer holidays.

We'd often get to Herne Bay early, have a walk around the town and buy some things for the pets and, as he was losing weight by then, some new clothes as well. There would be a couple of pit stops for a tea and something to eat before meeting up with Mark. But more or less an hour later, he'd be worried about missing the bus home so by half three we'd be heading back, getting home before five.

Home was always his sanctuary.

Home was where he felt safe.

Initially, when I first knew him, he had two keys for each lock on a single ring, but after a relapse, he gave me a set of keys so I could let myself in when I came round. This was handy as, up until the end of his dark period, if I hadn't had a set, no one would have seen him at all because he would often put the deadlock on and I was the only other person he knew who had a key for that. There would have been no way of making sure he had eaten or anything had I not had that set.

It was also handy as a couple of times when he was putting the rubbish out, he had the misfortune to lock himself out. One Sunday, I was still asleep when my buzzer went and at four in the morning this voice greeted me,

'Can I borrow your keys?'

'Stew?'

'I've locked myself out.'

'Hang on.'

I let him up and by the time he'd reached my door, I had the spare keys ready. He looked really worried as I asked,

'Want a drink or something before you go back?'

'No.'

So I gave him the keys, taking them back later that afternoon.

He also started to mislay them when we were heading out. He'd put them on the coffee table and then couldn't find them at first, partly because of all the other things that started to litter it, such as packet upon packet of spare batteries for his radio in the bedroom or the TV remotes, the fruit bowls, letters, glasses and mugs, but also because in not finding them first off, he'd get into a panic. Often, I'd find them, an inch away from where he'd been looking.

That's when he became obsessed with keys. It started innocently enough, or so it seemed, as he bought another key ring from the charity shop but then they had them in different colours so he brought the full range.

Then he went into the other shops and bought some more there, and then into the key cutting shop, where not only did he get some more chains, but also some more keys. These themselves could be patterned with football motifs and that sort of thing, so he bought a key in each of the patterns. It was like that childhood trend of collecting the discarded elastic bands the postman leaves and making them into a ball.

It did, however, make them much easier to find and he could always tell he had them with him, only shutting himself out once after this. Instead of taking the keys with him when he went to put some rubbish in the bin, he left the front door on the latch but the communal door caught the wind and shut on him. That at least was at a decent hour on a Sunday as I was already up that time. But having a huge bunch of chains weighing down his trouser pocket meant he struggled to get his wallet or bus pass out and with the crowds around him waiting to get on, it used to panic him a little.

This also created another unintended problem. If he was having one of his paranoid turns and needed to get in quickly as the panic attack took hold, he would struggle to find the key amongst all the rings and this would make him feel worse. Not so bad if I was there, coming to the rescue with my own set but on those occasions when he was on his own, I would come round to find he'd left his shopping bag with the newspaper and something from the charity shop in the hallway and was crashed out on the bed, keys on the telephone table, dumped there as he'd fled to the safety of his bed.

So I suggested he should thin the chain down and divide the keys between two sets. It sort of worked, in that he ended up with two sets of keys, but after a while this only led to him add more rings to both sets, including novelty rings and, as they became too big for his tracksuit pocket, he was forced to wear jeans whenever he went out and, as the pile of rings got ever fatter, he was having trouble getting them to even go into the pocket after a while.

Again, come the anxiety, come the panic, seeing his shaking hands struggle to find a key in the sea of key rings was heartbreaking, the panic made worse by having trouble getting the ball of keys out of his pocket.

Then I suggested the shoulder bag.

He had his cruiser bike by now and as I often had my rucksack on when I went into town, knowing they had side pockets, it seemed the natural compromise. With or without the bike, going to town with a rucksack on, even a one-strap, off-the-shoulder type, would have made shopping easier for him and he would also have had less chance of losing change from his pocket, hunting for the keys or trying to squeeze a hand past them all the time.

But he didn't like the idea of a rucksack, unless we were shopping or going for a picnic, unhappy about the way they hung round the shoulders. So I made another suggestion, a small satchel, expecting us to then look for one on the internet after our next shopping trip, but they sold bags at the key-cutting shop and he bought himself a small satchel to keep his keys, change, wallet, bus pass, that sort of thing, in, along with his earphones and MP3 player when on the bus.

Even cycling to bowling, Graveney or to The Sportsman, the large bag was fine, but the moment we started having picnics, with a rucksack as well, he found the large bag got in the way.

So in a very particular way, which I had to praise him for, he bought a smaller version to carry all he needed for when we went cycling, which on the 'Beastie Boy' rested more against the hip, making it easier than the original bag, that had always hung below the saddle.

So now he had a bag for town and a bag for cycling. As a result, he never had a problem finding his keys ever again and he had somewhere to put his lights and lock when we went shopping.

18

In fact, the satchels seemed to be the masterstroke that gave him the confidence to get out more. I'd see him come round for tea, large satchel slung over head and shoulder, trundling along the path, a quick wave, then round, or when in town myself, coming out of Gladstone Road, I'd suddenly hear the shout.

'Swiftly.'

Look round and there he'd be, briskly heading my way. We'd exchange a few words arranging to see each other later, then I'd ride on. Although by now, 'Swiftly' was a bit redundant as I was always on the cruiser bike.

He had two mobile phones, one he used all the time and one for back up if the other one ran out of power before he got home. He kept them along with all he needed in one simple bag, which he couldn't lose because he had to wear the strap like a sash and would only remove it when he was home. From the moment he had the phones his fear of what might happen receded. He even had less trouble finding his keys as he wasn't panicked trying to them in the first place and, as he became more relaxed even when we were out and about, he would be quite jokey.

As his confidence grew, his personality began to shine.

I noticed it return more quickly than everyone else as, at first, he became more himself at home, before becoming more relaxed out in social situations, so I saw the more gradual return of the happy little feller. His parents and Mark didn't see it so much until a year or so later and that was really because, as his confidence grew and he did more, he had more to tell them and had the confidence to have a conversation about his new-found interests.

When you've got nothing to look forward to and are just withdrawing into yourself, what can you say when someone asks you how your day was? But as soon as he had things to occupy his time, things which interested him and not things he was being forced into doing by some government-sponsored body, instead of listening to others about their lives, he actually said something back and took control of the conversation.

It had started with the food, telling his mum about what he was having. 'Tony's making a shepherd's pie.'

That sort of thing, but after a while the conversation would be.

'What you having for dinner, Mother? We had pasta with potatoes and green beans and some sauce on it. Tony made it. It's all fresh stuff..... Yeah, it was really nice..... Don't know what it's called, something foreign.... But it was really nice.'

As his confidence grew, he'd gone from standing in the doorway, watching and not really knowing what to do, into a routine which would start with, as I finished my tea, him clearing the top of the freezer. When Countdown's first game started, he'd join me in the kitchen, fetching the equipment and the ingredients, helping with the preparation, peeling and so on, then setting-up the two fold-away tables, getting the knives and forks, slicing some fresh bread, asking me for the butter before taking it all through to the tables. He would then be back to keep me company until the meal was almost ready, unless it was a risotto, then he'd be making up the second jug of stock whilst I'd continue to stir the rice.

At first I would have to remind him of the process,

'Right, if you set the table, knives and forks, and do some bread.'

'Right.'

But after a while,

'Okay, if you set the tables....'

'Done it.'

'Did you remember just a fork for me?'

'Yeah,' he'd say in a tired manner as if I'd said it too many times already.

'Cool.'

There was the occasional moody when he didn't want to set the tables or slice some bread and would moan about it, but reminding him that I was cooking and it would be a help would make him, with a grunt as he sort of understood, go and do these things. Anyway, from 2015, we always had bread on the table and he always set everything ready.

By then we had it to such a pattern that we could actually talk about things at the same time as I was cooking, nothing of any earth-shattering importance, usually about a forthcoming programme or some series we were watching, as we became like a team in the kitchen.

A sort of poor man's version of the 'Hairy Bikers', more like 'The Clean-shaven Cyclists'.

He was willing to try new foods and new styles, even if some fried chilli-spiced potatoes did send him out of the flat to recover, though strangely they didn't affect me. Most worked but some didn't. But on the whole, with the exception of only a couple of food experiments, most things he liked even if they were too rich and he couldn't finish them, regardless of everything now being small portions. He would even ask me to give him less, even if it was a chilli or pasta dish, and a meal that in the past would have served four now could be stretched to serve six.

He was getting out more, albeit to buy things from the charity shops. On a couple of occasions when we took the bus to the bowling alley, as we were waiting by one such shop, the manager saw him and they had a short conversation, something which only a year before Stewart had those satchels wouldn't have got past the first word. What struck me was she even knew his name so they'd obviously been talking during the times he'd visited her shop and he knew hers. He'd actually at some point had a conversation with her rather than just rushing in, finding something, paying and rushing out. I was impressed that so quickly his circle and his experiences were widening to a point where he wanted to improve his knowledge and experiences further than his original comfort zones.

He knew I was printing books as a new business venture and one weekend when we'd seen the first episode in the Hobbit trilogy, he told me he'd like to start reading again.

'Haven't you read any of the books you've got?' I asked, pointing over to the small book cabinet he had by his lounge door, in which I knew were a couple of the 'Harry Potter' books as well as a couple of Tom Clancy's.

'No.'

'How come? You've got a few.'

'They're too long. They go on a bit and I forget what's happening.'

'So you'd prefer a short book, like 'Planet of the Apes', or 'Fahrenheit 451?'

'Yeah.'

'We'll have to look up some next time we go shopping.'

A few moments passed and then he asked.

'You've published books, haven't you?'

'Well, they're not the sort of thing you'd like and one's a sort of children's book about a monster, although it's not a picture book. It's meant for older kids, ten plus that sort of thing, but it is a short story. Why? Do you want to read it?'

He nodded, so he did and he liked it so much he then bought his own copy.

He still didn't read the Potter or Clancy, but he did ask if I'd publish another 'Munch'.

'Can't really,' I told him. 'It's a one off.'

'Ow, I really enjoyed that bit where the creature kept being sick all the time.'

He meant where the creature kept eating all the people.

'But I could write another book for you if you like. What sort of book would you like?'

A bit of a pause as he thought about it.

'Pirates.'

'Okay, then I'll write you a comedy short story about pirates.'

So began a month's research into Calico Jack and other pirates in general. Using their history, but blending it in such a way that it became a parody of modern life and brought together pirates that probably didn't actually meet, helped me to weave a comic world around them. I began writing what was at first going to be another one off, until I was halfway through and I realised Calico and his crew could make a short series of little books for Stewart and other people with learning difficulties which would be fun for them to read.

Of course, Stewart was impatient to get the new book. But by the end of 2016 it was ready and he enjoyed it so much, he bought the next book, 'Waiting for a Train', as well, even though that was neither a comedy or a short.

He would read for half an hour each day, roughly a chapter for someone who found it difficult to read, and we'd talk a bit about each chapter each day and, as 2017 arrived, he would be badgering me again and again for another Calico Jack. I had already begun working on the next two, but I knew neither would be published before the end of that year.

He was also becoming more interested in things which obviously he liked but hadn't ever have had the chance to express a liking for before or been allowed to discuss before.

It started with 'Strictly Come Dancing', when during one show, he mentioned that he thought that one particular dance was very good, suffixed with his usual 'wasn't it' at the end as if he wasn't sure.

I agreed and thereafter every time we used to make comments about the dancing as we watched. He'd gone overnight from being a quiet passive viewer to someone who was actively thinking about and willing to discuss what he was watching. 'Bake Off', the old 'Crystal Maze' and other similar shows we'd talk about next, before we started exploring the sorts of things he would never have conceived of to watch previously, such as science and history programmes. Again we'd talk about them afterwards, probably not in as much depth, but he was now offering up questions and replies, whereas before, even before the dark times, if I'd made a comment about a show or anything, all I would have had in response was a 'Yeah', or a wordless grunt.

He was somewhat struck by the concept of the multiverse and particle physics in general but one thing I did notice that came up a lot in conversation, both in Strictly, but more often than not, during Countdown, was he would make a comment about Rachel's dress.

'That's a nice dress.'

or

'That's a bit 'how's your father'.'

'Think you're right there. She's only probably wearing that for a bet, unless she got dressed in the dark.'

He also like playing spot the mic battery, as on occasion,

Rachel's dresses being so tight, you could see the pack resting on her hip.

Often if he was looking for approval for liking something, he'd ask my opinion.

'Queen were a good band, weren't they?'

'Yes, they were.'

'I liked Queen, did you?'

'Yeah, think they were as good as the Beatles, if not better, really, as they didn't need to go all self-destructive to become inventive and interesting.'

'I liked them too.'

His developed interest in historical and mythological programmes became more critical and he lost interest in anything that didn't at least adhere to some resemblance of accuracy for that period in time. When it came to football, he wasn't just prepared to moan about the poor performance of an English men's team but would also offer up reasons as to why he thought they played so badly.

19

All these interests gave him something to talk about to his parents and to Mark. On the landline he would talk to his parents and he could be on the phone for ten minutes or more, a huge improvement from the minute or so he used to have.

He'd ask how they were, what they'd had to eat and then talk about one of the TV shows he knew they watched. If something like the women's football was on, or something else like the old 'Avengers' shows we'd found on an obscure channel, he'd tell them all about it and tell them they should be watching it too, but not in a dour, petulant way, but with all the vim and enthusiasm of a thirteen-year-old discovering something new for the first time.

He was enjoying life, albeit to the strict seven o'clock curfew, and was becoming more assertive, independent minded and mischievous in a gentle, jokey way.

He was prepared to justify his reasons for doing something in a logical, coherent way, that it was often hard to argue against, like when he'd just bought the smaller satchel, I had naturally assumed he was going to start buying bags in much the same way he had been buying DVDs and I had railed,

'What did you buy another bag for?'

'It's for on the bike. The other one's too big. It keeps getting in the way when I'm riding.'

Suddenly that made sense and so I'd concede.

'Fair enough.'

And that's all he used it for, decanting the phones and all he needed to that bag each night before we went shopping, bowling or wherever.

He also bought a trolley bag to use when he went shopping in town on his own so he didn't need to have carrier bags, even though he had a rucksack. He preferred to use that only on the Aldi shopping trips. He wasn't buying now just for buying's sake but because what he bought would make his life easier. As a result life in general was getting much easier.

Whenever he was in a jokey mood, or a little mischievous, more often than not when he'd done all his tasks and I was still cooking, he would go into either 'Wanna dance?' or 'Wanna fight?' mode.

'Wanna dance' was jokey, 'wanna fight' a little more mischievous, but both had the same starting point. He would stand there, hands pulled up to his shoulders, like jazz hands and a little bit of a sway for 'wanna dance', like a boxer but rooted still to the spot, for 'wanna fight', with dance leading to a series of jokes, normally at my expense, or fight mode, leading to a cheeky comment, often about something we'd seen or what was on the telly.

It was when he was in 'wanna dance' mode that he found out I was ticklish, when I had my back to him stirring a bolognaise. So sometimes if he was in that mood and I was sitting watching something as he came back from the kitchen, he would try and tickle me as he passed by, but he was easy to move on with a gentle prod up the backside from my boot.

When I was getting tired of the humour, the best way to signal that 'wanna dance' had run its course for the day was for me to roll my eyes and say under my breath, 'children', which he took in jest and quickly took it as the cue to settle down again before the fun turned into a manic episode.

In the same way, if I said something silly, often to get him thinking about something or to get a jokey reaction, he'd call me 'Hippie,' which he would also say if I was becoming too serious about something.

'Wanna fight' mode always ended the moment you changed

subject, so that was easy, but you always had to go through some silliness with 'wanna dance' to get it out of his system, which might explain why that mode only ever appeared in the safety of his flat.

You could tell his confidence had grown and he was better than before as he'd make more official phone calls, such as to BT, by himself only needing me to take over if he couldn't understand the accent. He also didn't just agree with people anymore. He was standing up for himself too.

This again was good to see.

His posture improved. He did still on occasion lie down to watch the TV, when bored by it. Most of the time, he sat upright, with a slight lean towards his 'secret stash of sweets' we all knew about but we didn't care about as he seldom ate them anymore. Because of this, the cat had to go from sitting on his chest to sitting on a set of cushions we'd put on the sofa between our two seats, or up on the windowsill.

Cycling was another confidence booster that brought out his personality as we'd go out more in good weather once I had my own 'Beastie Boy', also changing the way we'd all meet up before setting off.

Before then, if the three of us were heading somewhere, he and Mark would have met me around mine. I would then bring my bike down and we'd head off. However, if Mark was late for any reason or Stewart had had a relapse, I'd get a call to tell me to come round instead as we weren't going for a ride.

But when I had my own cruiser, we rode more without Mark, so I'd come round first to make sure he was ready. Then we'd both go round together to get my cruiser.

The first time I saw him bringing his bike down the stairs, a bike a third again the length of a mountain bike and nearly twice the weight, although only with a 19-inch frame, he was struggling. Its wheels were bumping on each step and there was a danger that one day he might lose control of it and end up going with it through the plate glass window at the foot of the stairwell. From then on I would always come round first, get his bike down for him and then we'd go and get mine, a system we repeated every time we went out and in reverse when we returned. It meant whenever he was riding somewhere, there was always going to be me with him, out there on our 'Beastie Boys', and it seemed to give him more courage to take the bike out more often, especially to Aldi.

Taking the 'Beastie Boys' shopping made a marked improvement on his health, which even he eventually noticed. When we'd first gone to Aldi, he'd struggled even on the flat, being out of condition from not riding since the previous summer, and it was a lot of stops and starts, but after a few weeks, only a couple of stops and one of them was to push the bikes up the hill.

With the reward of tea and a cake at the end of it, getting out on the bikes to go shopping wasn't a problem. In the beginning I would ride slightly ahead, leading the way. Even though he knew the way, he preferred it if I led and if I got too far in front, he would ring his bell and I would pull in and wait for him to catch up. Usually I'd look back and see he was taking a breather first but after a while, I'd look back and see I was just a bit too far ahead.

As he became more confident, we'd cycle side by side all the way there, making it fun, because we could talk at least until we had to go single file past the parked cars, but once off Faversham Road, it was side by side all the way there.

We had warm dry days only getting caught once by the rain. Our biggest problem at times really was that the wind was against us, making slow bikes even slower.

That said, after a few weeks, he'd noticed it was easier. He could get further without having to stop and on one extremely warm day in spring, he made it all the way to the bridge without having to stop. We both had to stop there as the bikes were too long to turn without having to put your foot down and scoot.

Cycling twice meant he was getting more than an hour's workout each week and as he felt healthier, he'd visit the town more, walk around there for half an hour three times a week, which helped with his stamina and his energy so that when we went out on the bikes for a picnic or just a ride along the seafront at Seasalter, he was able to keep up with me easily. He wasn't pedalling particularly hard anymore just to keep up. In fact, sometimes in the mirror I could see he was freewheeling as I wasn't going fast enough and on our way back he would lead.

With Stewart in front, we would keep a nice steady pace all the way. I didn't have to freewheel all the time to stay behind but could enjoy the ride too, just following, and he'd be no more out of breath at the end of the ride than I was. He wasn't anxious so wasn't panicked, or out of condition so wasn't exhausted, and he was enjoying it, as he would then tell his parents and Mark all about each trip, even if it was only to Aldi. They would hear how he'd cycled, what he'd bought, how long it had taken and how many stops he did or didn't make that time round.

Cycling had become fun, certainly more fun than it seemed those guys in those pelotons were having rushing by. We could enjoy the bird song, weave our way through the mobile dog chicanes and duck under the dragonflies, on a largely quiet, car-free route of cycle lanes to the shop, and a largely quiet, coastal road overlooking a thousand-acre marsh, free from the constraints of time, just doing our own thing.

It was no wonder he was getting happier.

He even started coming round to me more often, visiting almost daily once he had the satchel. He'd ring to ask if he could come round. More often than not it was fine and I'd then fill my kettle and get a couple of cups ready. I'd see him with his baseball cap and bag come along the path and look up at my kitchen window. He'd wave, I'd wave back and two minutes later, he'd arrive, with us going back afterwards to make dinner.

He would ring daily unless he was having a bit of a relapse. Those days he would take a lie-down in the afternoon and forget to ring, but they were so scarce now. I was having to clear my phone log each weekend because there were so many of his calls listed. It was running into a couple of pages a week.

He also became more able to express his feelings in his actions. Now when he had a drink, he would ask me if I wanted one or just make me one. Originally when he'd been getting his money from the Co-op, he'd have bought himself a biscuit, a sandwich or a cake. Then he started buying just the sandwich to share before buying us one each, even though he ended up, by 2017, seldom actually eating his own. Like the three TV magazines, he just couldn't stop the routine of buying us both one.

When he noticed that my key ring that had his keys on was a little past its prime, he went and bought me a Lego Batman key ring and, on another occasion, he got me a Hulk mug for my office to have my mid-morning coffee in, so I didn't have to use the same one I had my tea in.

20

Actually, at times, it became difficult to rein in his generosity, as with Christmas when it was his suggestion to have a meal at The Peter Cushing, we managed to organise it so Mark paid for the sweet and I paid for the extra drinks with a bag of crisps to share, but I'm sure if we hadn't suggested that arrangement, he'd probably have paid for the lot.

I was constantly telling him not to buy the doughnuts and the odd chocolate bar he'd buy me on occasions when he did replenish his 'secret store', but he took no notice and though he often said he'd read the newspaper he'd buy, I doubted he had because of the flyers. He was really only buying it for me, knowing I'd read it if it was there.

It was always as if he needed to make sure he'd spent all his benefits as soon as he could. I'm sure everyone on benefits is somewhat, by the rules imposed on them, forced to spend and save nothing. In a way that's good for the economy if no help to the individual, as it means they can never improve their situation as long as they're on it. However, as an economic driver, it's better than quantitative easing and, as the cuts bit, it's probably no surprise productivity, sales and the economy stalled as cutting benefits and giving money to the banks only helped house prices to stay too high and companies to buy things. No one had any money to buy anything they produced but by letting him get some enjoyment buying a newspaper or a doughnut for me meant he wasn't buying more DVDs or yet another biscuit barrel or other stuff to just sit and gather dust in his protective wall. If letting him get enjoyment from his 'gifts', despite some half-hearted protest to save his money, they were appreciated. If they didn't achieve anything else, they made him think more and take more time when in town as he was now thinking about other people rather than just himself.

However, he still never got the hang of budgeting, as always in the week he didn't get any benefit, he would by the weekend have run out of milk, cola and orange squash and would be borrowing the money from me to see him over until 'payday', when, after a trip to the Co-op, he'd give me the money back and I'd put it to one side again until next time.

Apart from the Christmas dinners, Stewart had always wanted to go out and try other places and, as my parents used to come down around May, though they only started doing that after my Nan died, I did invite him to come with me and my folks to The Long Reach to have a meal with us.

They were all in favour of the idea. They knew about him from our conversations and it would only have been the four of us but as we often didn't get back before five after seeing Nan's and Granddad's grave, dinner would have been at seven so it would have been tricky. However, despite all the progress, still not being comfortable meeting new people, he always declined, so sadly he never came with us.

But we did make it to The Peter Cushing a couple of times outside Christmas, for one of their steak dinners, the three of us, having dinner at around three and back by six.

On his forty-ninth birthday, there was a huge change, something up until then no one would have thought would happen.

It came about harmlessly enough. As usual, his parents asked him what he wanted for his birthday and, instead of the usual request for clothes, his confidence growing, his weight down and his general demeanour being a lot more sociable, he asked if he and I could go for dinner with them at this new place, The Oyster Bed in Swalecliffe, just them and him, and he wanted me there too and they agreed.

It was like most gastro-pub chains, a steakhouse, despite the seafood-sounding name and that was one thing he really loved, his steaks, and since he'd been on the diets and changed his lifestyle, he wasn't eating so many of them. I was probably only cooking them four times a year, instead of the twice a week he had when he cooked for himself, so a steak night seemed like the ideal present.

The food was nice, the drink and the company were nice but Stewart was a little nervous going and had to be excused from the table a couple of times, I suspect partly because of the diabetes but also because he had got himself all worried what the night was going to be like in unfamiliar surroundings.

They had put us on a back table, though near to another group. There weren't any noisy, loud children, music or anything else that might disturb the general ambiance and with me being able to hold a conversation for a couple of hours and still include him in it without him having to feel pressured into having to contribute, he relaxed and enjoyed the day.

I know as, for the next couple of weeks, he would mention it was fun, ask me constantly if I thought it was fun too, and say how much he liked the steak.

So, come the following year, a little thinner and with a lot more energy and a lot more confidence, he was asked again what he would like for his birthday and he asked for the meal again but this time to include me and Mark.

By now, Mark's mum was ill with Alzheimer's and he was afraid to leave her alone for more than an hour or two. The dinner was going to be at five o'clock, the same time as the previous year, and only us three and his parents would be going.

It was going to be the same place again. It was where Stewart wanted to go and, after being assured he didn't have to stay longer than the first course if he was really worried, Mark eventually confirmed he was definitely coming and the reservation was set for Tuesday 11 July, his actual birthday. Ironically, my birthday had fallen on a Tuesday and, strangely again, we had both been born on a Tuesday as well.

Tuesday's child is full of grace, the rhyme goes, and the grace in this case I think refers to God's favour rather than being graceful or elegant in appearance, though I think I'm elegant in my skinny jeans and shirts. Stewart's hoodie and tracksuit bottoms, his everyday casual style, were something of a contrast. As I had to pick up my new glasses that day at three, it was going to be a busy day for the pair of us.

So his fiftieth arrived and it rained.

Which at first might seem a bit bad for a birthday but it did mean when we got there, there weren't large numbers of people at the bar, getting drunk, and most of the tables were empty, so this time we were placed in a more central location, nearer the bar at a table that had a large curved sofa on one side and two chairs the other, making its own semi-snug. Stewart sat in the middle of the sofa, his mother and I taking the ends but, because we were a small party, we all had lots of room. You could have got another two around the table easily, which meant he could put his cap and satchel down, spread out, get comfortable and truly relax.

Mark was going to meet us there and we knew he might be a few minutes late, partly because of his mum and partly the weather being so bad as he was cycling down from Beltinge. While we waited, Stewart's dad, Graham ordered us all some drinks and then we were given a menu.

We were also told by the manager that he was a little short-staffed at the moment and he apologised in advance that the service was slow, which it was. It took five minutes before we got our drinks but, in a way, that helped too. It meant there wasn't any pressure to choose what we wanted to eat right away. No waitress breathing down our necks, hovering with electronic pen to iPad. We could take our time, read the menu, though Stewart had been going on for the past two weeks he was going to have a steak if it was still on the menu and was the only one of us who could have given his order as we'd walked in the door.

He had a bit of precedence for his concern, both The Long Reach and The Peter Cushing having changed their menus. The Oyster Bed had done so as well but it had become like The Long Reach, dumping most of the chicken options with plenty of steaks for him to choose from and he had a nice sirloin, but not the biggest on offer. He was getting healthier, he didn't eat such large portions anymore and of course he wanted the room for a sweet as well.

Mark turned up, just after the drinks arrived, looking a little soaked even with his plastic mac to protect him, and somehow he got his drink quicker than we had got ours. He apologised for being late and repeated he couldn't stay for long. Once he'd had enough time to look at the menu, we ordered.

I had the fish, as I wanted the rhubarb desert and needed to leave some space for it. Stewart had that as his sweet as well, and so, a couple more drinks later and after the first course, Mark was relaxed enough to stay for the sweet too, and by half seven we all left, Mark riding back to Beltinge and Stewart's parent's taking us back before heading home to Gravesend.

But his health and wellbeing were definitely improved. Not once did he have to slip away to the loo, not once did he not join in the conversation even though, like the year before, he didn't have to take over the conversation and be the centre of it at any time. No sooner were we in and the kettle on, he was already saying how much he'd enjoyed it, asking me several times if I had enjoyed it too, which he repeated for another couple of weeks.

That, for those couple of years was really the trick of a successful meal out, the numbers at the function. If the trend was to continue, then maybe come his fifty-first, he would have asked Robert to join us too, or maybe Anthony and Connor. At that rate anyway, by the time he would have been sixty, he might have well taken up one of his parents' invites to a barbecue in Gravesend.

On several occasions over the previous four years, Stewart had agreed to go when it was first put as being me, him, the parents and maybe Connor and Anthony. When the list was just that, he wanted to go. We'd sort out train times and work out our route to Gravesend but as soon as the number went over six, to included his more of the extended family, like Becky, Neal, Dan and so on, he'd start to get really anxious and he'd take steps to ensure that he couldn't make it, without having to lie to anyone.

He'd accidently on purpose spend the money he'd set aside for his rail ticket or panic if it was a Saturday, that there might be a lot of people on the train and say he couldn't sort out a ticket or ring up the Friday before and say he wasn't feeling well, which of course wasn't a lie. His agoraphobia was taking over making him feel all sick and ill, especially when he realised we were going to be picked up at the station and wouldn't be getting the train back until after the others had gone. Us not having control of when we might leave meant we might not have got back before seven. Looking at the train times, we wouldn't have anyway and that would make him panic before we'd even decided to go.

We even had the offer to go see his brother Dan for a birthday party at the Labour Club in Whitstable. With the reduced weekend bus schedule, it was only a thirty-minute walk away and anyway we were prepared to go halves on a taxi back. Even if we hadn't had any money left by the time we would have wanted to leave, it was a pretty straightforward journey home, but when he heard all Dan's work colleagues were going to be there, that was it, we couldn't go.

Too many strangers and too much noise.

If it had been the three of us to have a drink for Dan's birthday at the club, in a quiet corner, or at our own table, in the early afternoon and we'd been back by five or six, fine, but he just couldn't cope with the party and all those people. The idea of being as it were trapped in a room with people talking in groups but not necessarily talking to him made the paranoia demons just go into overdrive.

So the number of people at any event was important. Six or fewer it seemed he could cope and if he could get back by seven, he was happy too, even though he had got back later on his birthday bash, much to his own amazement. Seven was, when he was aware of the time, the cut of the moment, the time he wanted to be home by.

It always felt funny to go out for an afternoon, have a Christmas meal out and still be back for early evening telly, but at least it was something he could do and share with his friends.

Although never cured, and still somewhat anxious around people he didn't know, it would be fair to say that, for those four years in particular, he was managing his condition and enjoying living his life and it was food, fun TV, friendship, getting out and about, exercise and bikes that helped to do it.

21

It must have been the day after his birthday party or the day after that, that we were watching the telly and,

'Do you think I should get rid of some of my DVD's?' he suddenly said out of nowhere.

'Yeah, sure.' I was a bit surprised. 'Be a really good idea. Keep the ones you like and want to watch again, but get rid of the rest. Why? What's brought this on?'

'I was thinking of redecorating. Dad said he'd help but I've got to clear the room first.'

'Fair enough. Can't really paint round all the stuff on the shelves unless that's the look you're going for.'

He gave me that sideways grin as if to say, 'you're now being stupid'.

'Actually, you could probably get a bit of money back for them if you sell them online.'

'What? Enough to buy a computer?'

'Not sure you really need a computer. You don't really use them and if you want to check the price of something online, you can do that through your telly. You usually get me to order it for you anyway, so we might as well keep using mine. However, I noticed there's a hole in your bed.'

'Yeah.'

'Wouldn't it be better to get a new bed?'

'Yeah, suppose.' He shrugged, thought for a minute and then added, 'So how much do you think I could get for them?'

I looked around the room, thinking quickly how many there were. A quarter of them were horror films. With the exception of comic ones like 'Ghostbusters' and 'Tremors', I thought they could all go and replied, 'Two hundred, if they average at 25 pence each.'

'As much as that!'

'Enough at least for a new bed base. Might even get the mattress as well if we can get it in a sale.'

'Cool.'

'What we'll do, I'll bring my android round tomorrow. We'll set up an account and scan a few to see how it goes. Then we'll sort them out, get them into boxes and scan the lot in one go. Then I'll download the labels to my laptop and get them printed for you.'

'Can we do it all in one go?'

'Sure. Be several boxes but I'm sure we've got enough boxes between us.' Though I suspected that most the boxes in his box room were probably damaged under the weight of all those tool bags.

'We'll do that then,' he replied.

So the next day I brought a couple of boxes round, he'd found a couple too, and we started with the big pile behind the armchair. Well, it didn't take long to fill two boxes from that pile alone as most the films there were going. In the plastic tubs we emptied and sorted half of them until the rest of the boxes were full and in two of the tubs he had the ones he wanted to keep and two tubs were now empty.

Taking the smallest of the four boxes, we scanned the contents. The average film was between 20 and 25 pence, with one John Wayne film being worth nearer £2, but half that box was horror films and especially the cheap, nasty rip-offs of more famous 'slasher' films, were worth on the whole less than 10 pence each.

'Your bad horrors aren't worth much but I know there's not much horror in the big box and looking round the room, apart from that one rack and any more that are in those other tubs, most of the films worth ditching aren't going to be horrors anyway, so I think we're on track. We'll have to spend a weekend sorting the others out.

I'll have to find some more boxes. I think it's going to take a lot of boxes but I think it's going to work.'

'Okay.'

I therefore started to sort out some boxes, though I had to put some of them back together again first, so it meant a trip to Home Bargains for some parcel tape.

We were planning to start going through them after Saturday dinner. Then I'd bring the boxes round and we'd scan the pile as they went into the box Sunday instead of watching Columbo. But the plan got suspended four weeks as on 16 July, the Women's European Football competition started.

Channel 4 had made a big deal about it with their adverts and remembering the coverage from the Women's World Cup on the BBC, we were expecting the same level of coverage and to see every game. Even if it was moved on to a lesser channel, we were expecting the same level of coverage that you'd get for the men's game. But, of course, we didn't get it, because its women.

For the first week, we spent more time trying to find the games, trying to link up online which didn't work for some reason, and only catching the home nations' group games and the big knockout games on Channel 4 itself. So, for that first week, apart from the England and Scotland games, the main event of the tournament brought to you by Channel 4 was a documentary about how popular women's football was between 1918-1921 and their greatest team, Dick Kerr Ladies, a fine documentary but not really the football we wanted to see or what the ads had promised.

Despite this, Stewart's sparkle and zest for life were still there. He would ring Mark and even his parents to tell them when the England games were on and to try to get them to watch them too.

It also meant for the three weeks that the healthier lifestyle partly went out the window. Not so much the food, we were still buying the same dinners and including a lot of vegetables, but there was an increase in beer consumption, as when a game was actually televised, we would drink a can per half. Well, neither of us were big drinkers and that meant, before England's first match, against Scotland, we had to do a larger than normal shopping run.

Fortunately, it fell on a normal shopping day but it meant with all that extra beer, a pack of four per match and a run of four matches before the next shopping trip, taking the bikes was out the question. There was only enough space in the panniers for the beer and so we took a taxi, which in Stewart's reasoning would also include another for trip two, the M&S shop.

For the first and second of the next three weeks, we used the taxi to get our shopping. In fairness, the day of the second trip was a monsoon, so football competition or no football competition, neither of us wanted to cycle then but in the last week of the tournament with only three games left to play, the extra beer could have gone on the bikes. It only meant one more pack of four than we'd usually buy, so the day before I mentioned we should think about riding up again.

Rain was forecast but it was dry first thing and we could have made one trip before the rain did set in. However, he wasn't keen, wanting to buy some extra beer for the final on Sunday 6 August so we could have some beers with dinner as well.

So, as usual, before I came round, he went off early to our local Co-op to get the money for the taxi, pay his bills and get the sandwiches, magazines and so on.

The problem was the cash machine wasn't working so instead of waiting until I came round, he decided to walk all the way into Whitstable and back in less than an hour to get some money from another Co-op's cash machine.

I arrived at his place a few minutes after seven and found he wasn't there. I made a cup of tea and seeing there was no newspaper or TV guides I naturally assumed he was round our Co-op getting them, held up by some OAPs that might have got them before him.

I was about halfway through my tea, about quarter past, when I heard the front door open.

'I'm in here,' I called to let him know.

A moment passed. Then he came in, looking all hot and flustered, and carrying a small plastic bag in which were the usual magazines and so on.

'Bet you wondered where I was, didn't you?'

'Down the Co-op. I noticed the paper wasn't here. What was it? A long queue or something.'

'No.' He disappeared into the kitchen to return with a squash.

'The cash machine isn't working. I went down to the Co-op by the bridge to get the money for the taxi.'

I had to laugh. 'I'm not laughing at you, Stew. It's just, you do realise it would have be easier to wait until I got here and we could have walked up to Aldi together. They've got a machine up there, inside. We could have got a taxi back.'

'I know.' He grinned as he began to see the absurdity of what he'd just done.

'Only it's only a mile to Aldi, okay, uphill, but you realise you've just done three miles to save doing a mile? That's what's funny.'

'I know. What am I like!' He started to laugh.

'Got to admit, you won't need to cycle today. Whatever, you've done more exercise getting there and back so quickly than you would have done if we'd ridden up there four times!'

'Yeah, but.' He could see the comic irony too. 'I'll call a taxi.' He started to get the phone out of his satchel.

'I've not finished my tea yet.'

'Well, hurry up then.'

That football final week, with the kids off school and the weather being so bad, we didn't go bowling either so he hadn't been on the bike for nearly a month, though, he was still getting things for the bike, looking forward to riding it again now the summer was here.

He was planning to get the indicators with the next shop, we'd order online at Amazon, and wanted yet more lights. Some clothes he'd ordered, two new hoodies and some trainers had just arrived and he was looking forward to wearing them on our soon-to-be-had trip to The Freewheel.

But it was also that football final week that he started to hold his jaw more and I wondered if he'd chipped a tooth or had toothache. Holding his jaw, resting his elbow on the other arm whilst doing so, wasn't that uncommon. It was his default pose when almost sitting upright, so when he said he didn't have a problem, I didn't think much more about it.

But, by the football final, I did notice, however, he was drinking more cola than usual and the full sugar stuff again, not the sugar free, but it wasn't until that Sunday that I noticed he was making a bit of saliva in his mouth and that his tongue would come out of the side of his mouth as if he was trying to keep something away from a hole in a tooth or something like that.

Or that's how I interpreted it. He was eating a bit less than usual but he didn't seem to be having any difficulty eating. He wasn't eating on only one side of his mouth, like I would if a filling or a tooth hurting. He just didn't seem so hungry and I guessed he was like me full of beer and just didn't really want too much to eat.

Since using only the willow-patterned plates, he was now eating what any dietician would call a sensible amount. Only from the quarter finals did we drink more than two cans a day as there were more than two games in a day, so four beers in four and a half hours, twice a week. You couldn't say that those two days were excessive either, taken over the course of that week.

Though for the final, we did overdo it a bit, drinking two cans per half plus two beers for dinner. Well, it was the final.

But I asked him again if he had a bad tooth on Monday the 7th and offered to take him to my dentist's surgery if he didn't want to use his usual surgery. I would have even given him my space and put mine back a few months if it would have helped, but he said he was okay.

On the 7th and 8th, he rang me at around quarter past one, to ask me to come round to his for coffee. Monday's call lasted 53 seconds and Tuesday's 47, which were normal when he asked me to come round to his for a drink. Working from five in the mornings, I was often finished by one, so it was no problem. His calls were only longer usually at night when I'd just got back home or in the mid-morning when he wanted a chat.

He seemed fine, was as chirpy as ever and, when I left later at around nine, nothing seemed out of the ordinary.

He didn't have to ring me on Wednesday as we were going shopping and I'd do a few hours in the afternoon at his place. It was the one day in the week, as we had been doing all that year, when I stayed longer than I did on a Sunday and we spent the whole day together.

The only thing different about him I noticed those three days was the saliva thing hadn't gone away.

On the Wednesday, we took a taxi again. We agreed this would the last taxi run unless it was raining a monsoon, not because we couldn't afford £3 between us, but as it was getting warmer, summer seemed to be returning. It was a shame to waste the bikes and really we were only taking this trip because he wanted to buy some extra things for the freezer as the football had used up all the chips and we wanted some more dine-in-for-twos and some wine from Aldi.

We also agreed while we were waiting for the taxi that we should go for a picnic, the fifth and last for the year, the day after the August

Bank Holiday as then it should have been quieter, so we took the taxi to Aldi and went into M&S to have our tea and cake.

I ordered and paid for the two teas and two apple turnovers as our usual Eccles cakes weren't there. He went down to the window tables, taking his usual place, with his back to Sheppey so he could see the car park and Aldi entrance, and shortly afterwards I joined him.

I passed the cups and turnovers and as I handed out the serviettes, he placed his mini Abbey crunch from his saucer to mine. Then he found his trolley token which he put ready by his cup.

I'd just started to eat my apple turnover when after two bites he put his down on the plate and pushed it away.

'Don't you want it?' I asked.

'Tastes funny,' he replied.

I ate mine and it seemed okay but then to me a turnover's a turnover. It might have been a bit over baked but nothing I noticed.

'Do you want mine?' he asked. I did consider it. I hate wasting food, but we were going to have a takeaway that night, the one bad day of the diet that justified all those salads and meat substitutes, and as my stomach had also shrunk a bit over the past couple of years I replied,

'No, don't worry about it. Do you want me to get you something else?'

'No, I'm not really hungry,' he replied.

Then as I emptied the teapot and started to sip my tea, he was putting his satchel over his head and shoulder.

'Come on then.'

'I'm drinking my tea.'

'Well, hurry up then.'

At Aldi we did bulk up on wine for Sunday dinners. That is, we bought two clarets, knowing we were going to get two dine-in-for-twos at M&S and so would have a couple of bottles then.

He also wanted to try some Prosecco. His sisters had gone on about always drinking it and as he'd never had anything like champagne, we got a bottle of that too.

The plan was to have it that Saturday with a film, the last instalment of the Hobbit series, The Battle of the Five Armies, as at last it was being screened.

As we waited outside Aldi for the taxi, two bags for life, two rucksacks and the pull-along trolley all full to overflowing, he took up his stance.

'Wanna fight?' And again I noticed there was the familiar sound of saliva being drawn over his teeth as he grinned at me. Something had to be the problem and I wondered if that was why he hadn't wanted his turnover.

'You sure you haven't got a bad tooth.'

'Hippie.'

'Look, man. I just want you to be happy and look after yourself, okay?'

He nodded. 'Okay.'

'If there's anything wrong, you'd tell me, right?'

He nodded.

'And that includes your teeth, right?'

'Yes, dad.'

I rolled my eyes. 'Children.'

We waited a little while and then I made a comment about the trolleys for people in wheelchairs, having noticed for the first time that they had a grip to hold them to the chair, and then our taxi turned up.

The second trip to M&S was good. We only had a tea that time and as we didn't go anywhere else, we found a nice meal to put away in the freezer including a pudding and one Mediterranean meal to have that Sunday, oh, and two bottles of wine, this time one white and one rosé, along with the four we already had. We now had eight and a sparkling wine for Saturday.

We had fish and chips that evening. He had his now normal children's portion but he didn't eat all of that either. To be fair, I struggled too. Those turnovers it turns out can be really filling. The only thing we didn't do as planned was to buy the indicators or start scanning the DVDs, deciding to leave that all to Sunday as now our Sundays were going to be a bit quiet on the TV until 'Strictly' started again. I left at our normal time and everything seemed normal.

He didn't ring me on Thursday, which I didn't think too much about. With all the excitement of the football and now all the bad weather and less exercise for nearly a month, I assumed that he was probably having a minor relapse and it would take a week or so until he was back to a happy balance.

When I came round in time for a tea before Rachel, I found him dressed so he'd been up in the day, and he had bought a paper, but was lying on the bed asleep.

I noticed at dinner he was knocking back the cola and left his bread but did eat all the salad. That again hadn't been uncommon as this year had progressed, though we still did bread with a light meal like a salad. Since May, he'd throw most the bread away, making two slices, eating only half of one.

Friday, again no call during the day and he wasn't on the bed this time when I arrived, but had just gone into the lounge and was about to ring me. He looked a bit tired and worn so I guessed he had been for a lie down during the afternoon and had probably rung Mark or his parents first before planning to ring me.

He was though, a little unsteady, more clumsy than usual, in that he walked into a couple of things.

He seemed a bit anxious and I told him, 'If you're worried about something or there's a problem, you can tell me you know,' adding, 'I just want you to be happy, that's all.'

He smiled briefly and I stayed to watch The A-Team through to the Honor Blackman Avengers and I left at my normal time, it being just a normal evening otherwise.

22

He was still making a wet saliva, had been for two weeks now, but he was telling me he felt fine in himself. He still seemed fine. He'd seemed fine shopping and though Thursday and Friday he'd been taking a nap in the afternoon, that wasn't unusual for him. He would do that if he felt a little down and withdrawn and now the women's football had ended and Strictly was still weeks away, he was probably, in my experience of the past six years, just having a pause period, a small relapse as he worried what the next series would be like in two weeks' time. Once we'd started cycling again, he would be back to his good old self.

I was always mindful of his heart and the diabetes, which was why I wouldn't push him to ride further than he could manage and was glad the old mountain bike was gone but the shakiness and the fatigue were making me wonder if the diabetes was getting worse.

It was confusing me as there was always a danger of the condition getting worse all the time he was over 42 inches but he was more active and eating a lot more healthily, even to the point where he hardly ever had either olive oil or cheese in his diet either, so I couldn't see how the condition could be getting worse. I accepted that the football had meant a bit more beer than usual but that had been the only 'bad' thing added to our diet in a month and without any pizzas or anything like that, we'd still maintained the healthy diet we'd had before so it shouldn't have been a factor.

I was concerned about him. He kept touching his lips as if he was worried by something. Problem was, he was up to date with his bills. Yes, he had one to pay the next week but he was sticking to budget and paying things normally ahead of time so he was well up to date. I couldn't see what he could be anxious about.

Then I remembered he was drinking more cola. If he had a tooth problem and was bulking up on the sugar again, to avoid eating for two weeks, maybe the body was having a

diabetic episode.

Because it was the only conclusion I could come up with. Saturday seemed to prove I was right when he bumped into things and seemed even more clumsy than usual. After dinner with a bit more bread with it, he went to bed early. The football season had just started but the first couple of weeks weren't that important. I told him as I left early if he had a problem to ring me. He said he would, he had his phone by him and I left him to sleep it off.

Sunday 13 August was pretty much like any other day. I Skyped my parents and I turned up as normal, only to find Stew still in bed.

For a Sunday that wasn't uncommon and I wasn't unduly concerned. However, saying that, since Aldi had opened, he had normally been up when I arrived.

This time though he was very shaky when he sat up. Quickly, fearing he was nearing a diabetic coma or passing out episode again, I went to his stash of sweets and found a Snickers bar which I gave him to eat.

Dinner being Italian was a high carbohydrate meal, a pasta bake with bread followed by almond tarts, all which he ate apart from some of his pasta bake.

By four he wasn't shaking any more at all. He'd been shaking less as the day went on, though he was still tired. In himself he seemed happy. He was in high spirits and looking forward to Monday's dinner, which I knew he'd like a lot, Scotch egg with baked potato and baked beans, and Tuesday our next shopping day.

He went to bed early as I watched the end of the Columbo and I asked him just as I was going to leave,

'You be alright now and rest.'

'Yes.'

'If you feel shaky, give me a ring. Don't do anything. Give me a ring and I'll be right over, alright?'

'I will.'

'Sure you're okay?'

He nodded and added, 'Yes.'

'You get some rest.'

I then went home, watched Ed Wood and then went to bed. Again, I wasn't particularly concerned. It seemed we'd arrested a diabetic attack and I was sure, once we were back on the healthy diet and less beer, he would be back to normal.

*

So on Monday 14 August 2017 I woke, not too enthusiastic about the day ahead as I still had another book to finish. I wanted to have two ready for printing in 2018. I couldn't do what I had planned as my funding arrangements had changed and I now had only half as much as expected to operate with. The two replacements were taking a bit of time to complete. I had ready to send to the proofreader the second in the Calico Jack Series, which I wanted to come out closer to Christmas, along with Mandy, the first of the two replacements and now a final read-through short of being ready, which I was planning to bring out in February.

Calico had to be ready for Christmas so Stew would have something to read when I was away over the holidays. I was planning to send it off in September, needing three months to let the proofreader correct it, make the corrections, set it, design the cover and then send it to print. I couldn't do it before as the replacement works had precedence.

So I went round a little earlier than usual, convincing myself that a good spud takes two hours to cook and was ready for another night of dinner and old telly.

It was a bright late afternoon, not cold, but not great considering it was summer and I needed a light jacket as I made my way round as normal.

As I opened the door, I could see the bedroom light was on and that the lounge door was shut which at first I took to mean he'd been late getting up and had just popped out for a paper, having probably knocked the light on as he left. It wouldn't have been the first time I'd found the flat like this, lights on in the afternoon and for a second I assumed he must be feeling a lot better or else he wouldn't have gone out.

It was then that I glanced into the bathroom and had the shock of my life.

He was knelt down by the toilet, his face on large unopened packet of toilet rolls we'd got from Home Bargains only the last week and his arms were slumped at his side, fingers curled but with the palms outwards. He was dressed in his night clothes and to me it looked like he'd just got up.

Instantly I thought he'd had one of his diabetic episodes, hadn't eaten all day, and that this was one of the same comas I'd found him in all those years ago.

Now as then, at first I thought a few taps on the face and calling his name would revive him but as I pulled him back, I suddenly noticed the blood all over his face, forehead to nose. It was like he was wearing a mask.

I checked.

He wasn't breathing.

I laid him flat and noticed he had blood coming out of his belly button.

I shot into the lounge for the house phone and dialled 999. It got rather hectic for a bit. For one I wasn't used to the phone and its curved ergonomic design which, though good for just sitting around talking, isn't good when you're trying to give your best friend CPR and talk to the emergency operator as I got cut off twice but fortunately, they rang me back each time.

The first guy, at a division in Liverpool, I'm sad to say I think I swore at when he asked me for a third time what service I needed and I told him in no uncertain terms I wanted an ambulance. Also, you get to realise in that situation as the person dealing with you has no local knowledge, it feels it takes an age to get all the address details across.

But he passed me to another person, a woman this time, and she kept me on the line. Again, we lost the connection for a moment but she got back to me and went through the CPR thing with me.

I'd learnt how to do it, both with the Cub Scouts and the ATC, but it had changed a little since then. You didn't have to breathe into a person anymore and also the pumping rhythm had increased. Both I knew and, fortunately, those skills had kicked in instinctively and I was doing it right. She told me not to worry about pressing down hard and to come beside him to do it, both of which I was already doing, but it doesn't hurt to be reminded in such a situation. She also wanted me to say 'one and two and three and four' continuously down the phone, which I rested on the bath, knocking over most of Stew's shampoos and bubble baths at the same time.

I pressed and pressed. He bounced with every press and I was sure I was going to break his ribs and could just hear him moaning for the next fifteen years about how I'd broken them.

But I could live with that.

I had been going for longer than ten minutes.

I was beginning to tire when I heard a siren and in a very short time I opened the door to three fire officers, the first responders, who then took charge and I went to sit in the bedroom watching.

It was then I saw the clock, twenty past two. Everything had happened in twenty minutes.

At this stage I was still hopeful. I'd seen the blood on the tissues, the blood on his face, and now there was blood on the floor, but I was still hopeful. The blood was still wet. I noticed I had some on my jeans and would later find I had his blood on my canvas shoes and my jacket sleeve. So he had to be alright. I mean, this was Stew, he was four months younger than me. He couldn't die. We'd always joked I'd be the first to go because I was older.

Then the first fireman said he was cold. In all my panic to save him I'd not noticed he was cold, well, maybe a bit cold, hard to say. The urgency had taken over and I think I was sweating anyway so touching him, he hadn't felt cold to me.

They used a thermometer in his ear and it was true. He was cold.

He was dead.

It was then I went completely numb.

The NHS ambulance team arrived probably no more than five minutes later. Two female paramedics entered, Becky and Laura, I think their name badges read. It's funny but for a moment a gentle calm seemed to overtake me as they took over and the firemen expressed his sympathy to me and left.

But I was still numb, in shock I suppose, but at that time didn't know it and after the two paramedics had done their stuff and filled in their forms, the first asked me if I wanted a cup of tea.

I knew where everything was and volunteered to make it, only for her then to say we couldn't make it in Stewart's place. The police were on their way and we were to touch nothing.

I began to shake.

I didn't want to leave the little feller. I didn't want him to be alone but they thought it was best I went down to the ambulance.

I had to leave Stewart behind.

*

I sat in a chair, opposite the long stretcher bed and Laura gave me a little disposable cup of water. Again, like the firemen and the people on the phone, they asked me Stewart's name which I gave and then mine. Then they asked me about him and his medication, which I couldn't remember the names of, only what they were for, how he was feeling and why I was round and so forth.

I explained it all calmly and as soon as the silence returned, I started to cry.

She comforted me but the pain was overwhelming and it took a little while before I could stop. Everyone was concerned that I had someone to talk to that night and wanted to know where my family and friends were. His next of kin were in Gravesend, mine are in Wales, and they wanted me to have someone closer around, just in case. We needed to contact Mark.

The police arrived and asked the same questions as well as if he had any enemies.

Enemies? Demons, but nothing we couldn't cope with. But no actual enemies.

They were looking for his next of kin to contact. I knew their numbers were on his phones but on the house phone no numbers were listed and at first no one could get into his mobiles because he had locked them with a pin code.

The police tried his date of birth. They and the paramedics tried obvious combinations and then they gave it to me. At first I couldn't think. For a moment then I would have struggled to spell my own name and after a few moments of groggy-minded attempts, I paused and thought about Stewart.

Then it hit me. He was never good with numbers. He was always asking me to do the sums and I realised, if he'd taken my advice, he would have put a number in that was easy for him to remember.

I pressed, 1,1,1,1.

Okay.

It unlocked and I was in.

I had to smile and then that made me cry again for a moment. Gathering my strength, I took the phone to the police but his parents' number was not on there either, well, not listed in the contacts and of all the numbers rung, other than my own, I knew the other mobile was Mark's.

I also told the policewoman about Stewart's address book. I knew the numbers would be in that and I also told them that his parents didn't have the same surname as Stewart but again, for a moment I couldn't think what it was even though I knew I knew it. They found some names and mentioned Stevens, which was it.

They tried it but they were out.

I hoped they were out and not on holiday. Stewart hadn't said they were on holiday. In fact, I could recall they'd not long been back from one when we'd been to his birthday meal.

They arranged for the coroner to come, who duly arrived, and they took my best mate to the Queen Elizabeth The Queen Mother Hospital in Margate to work out how it was he died.

The post mortem.

They also said they'd leave some food out for the cat and that they would contact me again by phone, either later that night or the next day, and that one of them would come round later to drop off my keys, or rather my copy of Stewart's keys, back to me.

It wasn't not so much the keys I wanted, it was the ring, although I guessed until his mum and dad could come down to sort out the property, I was going to have to feed the cat and bird and would also have to let them in, as at this stage, no one else had their own set.

But I wanted the key ring more than anything else. He'd bought it for me in one of his impulsive moments and I wanted it back. It's only a Lego Batman but it's not the value of something, the amount spent, but what it signifies. He was a real friend and you only get one or two of them in your whole life.

In the back of the ambulance we rang Mark now the police at least knew where to find his next of kin, though I couldn't tell him without breaking down again so Laura took over.

At this moment in time, the realisation he was gone was just dawning on me and it hurt, it really hurt so much, I couldn't stop crying.

The policeman returned and told me there was nothing I could have done, that I'd been a good friend to Stew, and then the ambulance team drove me around the block and home, where they made me a cup of tea, and made sure I was alright before they left.

For a moment I was angry and cried.

I was angry he was gone, angry that he'd died before he'd tried his bottle of champagne and then so sad. I couldn't stop crying because I was never going to see him ever again.

No more talking about the football, no more manic shopping trips to Aldi, no more whining about going on a bike ride, then going riding and having a picnic by the sea anyway. All that had been stolen from us, the simple joys. Suddenly of all the things I've done over the decades, it was those little things with him, be it Strictly or Match of the Day or an umpteenth repeat of Columbo, enjoyed together that we were never going to share anymore.

No more special Sunday dinners, no more trying out the recipes from my cook book and no one to make my own special curry for, no more curry days.

I was beginning to despair and then my doorbell rang.

The keys were returned.

I was told he had been picked up and was reminded that I should be contacted by the police later that day or the next day.

I wish I could have gone with him but I guess that's not what happens.

There were two missed calls, no number, on my phone when I returned. I'd been outside with the policewoman so had missed them. I knew if it was the police, they'd ring back the next day, so too if it was Sue and Graham. Then, with my tea, I waited for Mark to ring.

He was later than he said he would be. He'd needed time to come to terms with it too, to get over the shock.

That I could understand.

The shock hadn't been in how I found my dear mate but in the loss of him himself.

We talked for a few minutes then agreed to meet up the next day in Stewart's favourite pub, The Peter Cushing.

It was a natural choice.

Afterwards, I Skyped my folks, agreeing to talk to them again the next day after seeing Mark, and decided I'd go to the doctors to see about some counselling on Wednesday.

When my grandparents had died four years apart from each other, though it had been expected, I hadn't talked to anyone but Stewart about them and it had taken a year in each case to get over them. This time it was different. The pain was so much stronger so I was determined to take the paramedic's advice and seek help this time.

I took Dad's advice and put some sugar in my next cup of tea. Normally, I can't drink a cup if it's got a single grain of the stuff in it but strangely it didn't taste sweet until I'd put three cubes in. As I didn't feel like cooking much, I had a pizza, which I struggled to eat but managed to, and watched a film we both enjoyed, 'The Naked Gun'.

After that, I needed something to do, something to remember him by, the good times and the bad, the whole package and so that same night, I started writing about him. Everything else, all the other projects could wait until September, after I'd come back from Wales, as I also decided there and then I was going to spend a couple of weeks away after the funeral.

Calico Jack the second, Sam Bishop, Mandy and The Twisted World of Lisa Hepburn could wait.

23

I didn't sleep at all that night and in the morning I went round to Stewart's, fed the bird, and checked on the cat, which was still hiding in his wardrobe.

When I got home I had another cry, then his parents rang. They were coming down and so I arranged to see them later and I contacted Mark. We were going to meet at two, though he rang later to make it half past.

I was keeping myself busy when the police rang, thanking me for staying behind, expressing regret for meeting under such unhappy circumstances, and saying that without my help that they wouldn't have even found his next of kin and that I had been a good friend to him.

When Sue and Graham arrived, at first they were a little surprised by the disorder of his place. In fairness to Stewart, a lot of the mess, especially the discarded things on the floor and the stuff knocked over in the bathroom and lounge, was down to me in my haste for the phone, administering the CPR and so forth. However, the general untidiness was a symptom of his earlier deep depression and his general mental illness, made worse by his pills which actively suppressed his energy and thought processes in order to manage his illness and, though it was untidy, it was still a managed untidiness. The areas he actually lived in were kept clean.

The fruit had gone off. That day was supposed to be our shopping day and he always bought more than he needed. Then they saw the pile of cakes and biscuits and for a moment thought that was what he was eating until they saw the dates on them, some over three months out of date. Like I said, he may have been buying them but, with the dinners and change of lifestyle, he wasn't eating them.

Then Graham and Stewart's brother Dan went to catch the cat, still in the wardrobe, not having been out since the moment I came round the afternoon before.

Can't blame the cat really. He had a blanket and his favourite toys in there and since Stewart had had him, we'd let him have that place as his bolthole, the place he could go to when life was too stressful for him and which was normally a human no-go area.

Now that bolthole was going to be torn away from him, but not without a fight. He clawed his initial escape only to be captured behind the freezer. He was eventually put into the cat box and Dan started the process of trying to find somewhere to re-home him. That's when I left to get ready to meet up with Mark. Jason was a good cat. He just didn't like being held but wasn't spiteful or anything and I was sure they'd find somewhere to re-home him but they hadn't done so by the time we saw them later at The Peter Cushing.

I met Mark outside. To be honest, I didn't feel I could go in and wait on my own without remembering all the good times there with Stewart. I'd only ever been in there with him before. Mark was ten minutes late. I'd been an hour early, though I'd needed the walk and had spent my time walking around the town, seeing it differently for once.

It was high season but strangely quiet this year. Maybe it was the reduced Oyster Festival or maybe because it was such a hot day, everyone was down at The Slopes. I've cycled that way many a time on a hot day and have had to weave my way through so many people it was like doing my cycling proficiency test through the cones all over again, but over two miles.

We talked, saw Sue, Graham and Dan, who'd gone there for something to eat before his parents headed back to Gravesend for the night. They left us to ourselves as we reminisced.

Mark was saying he was upset with himself for not visiting

Stewart at the flat since last year and not joining us on a bike ride. But the only reason he hadn't been round was that he was now full-time carer for his mum and, without the provision of home visits from any trained care assistants to help him, he had to do it all by himself.

Stewart and I knew this. It didn't mean anything to us but he was still sorry he hadn't been round. He was, however, so glad he'd come to Stewart's 50th birthday bash, remembering how happy Stew had been with us all there. Mark had been sitting opposite him so he would know how involved Stewart had been. He'd not known him so relaxed out and about before.

I knew this was true.

Stewart had gone on about it being a great night for two or three nights afterwards and, once the kids were all back at school, wanted us three to go there on a meal-deal night, just the three of us, and I think, cycling aside, we would have done.

Before he had his own flood of tears and when I bought the round, Mark said,

'I'd known Stewart since 1997, twenty years, and I never knew him half as well as you. When I knew him he was withdrawn, lonely, but over the last years Stewart was really happy and interested in things, like movies, reading, food, even women's football because of you. He was like a zealot at times, ringing me up, saying you should watch this game during the Women's Euros, and I would pretend I was going to, but that was because of you, that was because of you, you made his life interesting. I mean, you're two very different people. You've been to university and he had a hard life before he went into foster care. He was treated really badly and obviously he didn't go to uni, and yet, you're two people who clicked. You got him interested in different things too. If you hadn't had met him and made him happy, he would have done himself some harm and, who knows, he probably wouldn't have lived past 2005, I met him a couple of weeks after he first moved on to the estate. He'd painted his rooms, that sort of thing, but he was feeling isolated, wanted to move, and I don't think where he moved to, it would have been any different. I'm sure he would have self-harmed himself again if it wasn't for you. You've given him thirteen years of happiness, you should be proud of that.'

*

I walked home. As I turned onto Joy Lane, I got a text from Mum asking if I wanted to Skype and replied I'd be half an hour.

Shorter talk this time. They said I looked tired. Well, I had been awake now continuously since 04:03 Monday the 14th. It was now 18:45 on Tuesday the 15th, and from the moment they said I looked a little tired, I thought, yes, I was, so I had something to eat, a leftover Lasagne I'd frozen.

I ate dinner watching an episode of Dad's Army, was then going to watch something else, got five minutes into it but suddenly became so tired that, at a quarter to eight that night, I put the clock radio on to sixty-minute snooze, listened to a couple of songs, heard the news, then another song and the next minute I knew it was 04:30 on Wednesday morning.

24

Waiting to hear the outcome of the post-mortem and knowing that Stewart was slowly being erased from society as his parents cancelled his phone, broadband, water bills, TV licence and so on was killing me and, for the whole morning, every time I thought about him and remembered one of his idiosyncrasies I began to cry.

It was heartbreaking, I felt lost, not just feeling for my loss, but actually had lost myself as I couldn't seem to function at anything at all. Even making a cup of tea was difficult and it hurt, physically hurt. My head hurt from all the crying, my body ached and I felt so, so sad.

I had three teas with sugar in them to keep my strength up and I hate sugar in tea. I only keep the cubes for when my Dad visits. Stewart used to have sugar in his coffee but I weaned him off it.

I listened to the radio, cleared up around my place and basically carried on, though I couldn't get any work done, couldn't concentrate.

Inside I still suffered the pain. There was a harsh pain that wouldn't go and my body felt like lead.

There are moments that bring it all back with a vengeance. Like when I'm standing by my kitchen window making a cup of tea and I look down to the path between the gardens of two sets of flats, the route he'd take if he was coming to see me, coming round for a coffee or a tea. He would come this way and I'd see him, wave and he'd wave back, him in his baseball cap and in the last couple of years, with his bag round his shoulder, making his way to me.

That was the only reason to look out of that window, on the off chance, just in case, and now, well, I still can't help looking out for him, on the off chance, and then I remember it's never going to happen again, and again I'm crying.

Twelve years he came that way and every time, he'd look up and wave. Probably because he knew that I'd be filling the kettle, making the drink as he headed over, especially if he'd rung first, and liked the idea that I was looking out for him and would wave. Who knows?

But it was the way he'd always come and he won't be coming that way anymore.

For the most part of the day, I would become upset at the slightest thing. I knew Graham and Sue were coming down later in the day and, although they had his keys, I was expecting them to ring me and let me know, possibly to help go through things.

In a way, I'm glad they came down and carried on without me as I'm not sure going back to the flat I would have been able to cope. Every reminder at the moment brings me to tears, and although I can keep it together or at least did yesterday in other people's company, in the morning of that first day after, when I had gone round to feed the cat and bird, it had been all too much and so although I was waiting to hear the result of the post-mortem, staying busy in my own flat was easier.

I slept that night, but not as long as before and it took a bit of time to nod off. I did, however, find watching Red Dwarf XI, a series we'd shared together, was therapeutic for me, laughing at the same jokes and recalling how excited by the return of the series he'd been and how it hadn't disappointed us in anyway made me deliriously happy for the rest of that night. Though I had thoughts about him as I tried to drift off, it was only of the chirpy little chap that surfaced, even to the point of hearing some of the comments he'd made, like, 'That Rimmer's Crazy,' and 'That was really funny him having his head printed like that', or 'The Cat was good', came flooding back and for that night at least, he was still alive.

25

Wet day today, the 17th, and I hope soon I'll know how why it all happened as it's the uncertainly of it all that's now eating away at me.

I had given myself an itinerary of things to do, things I needed to do and so I wasn't going to end up just dwelling on all that had happened. Well, for the most part that worked. There were still a couple of sad moments, when I had to let myself have a little cry.

Got a call at 08:35 from Graham. The coroner had rung but the cause of death was still unknown so they were sending samples off for toxicology, for blood tests, that sort of thing, and that was going to take about eight weeks but everyone was satisfied there were no foul means involved so he was granting Graham an interim certificate which would allow them to have him cremated.

The funeral arrangements were going to take place down in Margate and they were going to start that process later today after they'd been to the flat. A skip was coming round on the Monday to collect all the stuff of his that wasn't worth doing anything with.

The main extended family were coming down. Even though I offered to help, I'm glad in a way they refused it as I still didn't want to go back into his flat and knowing this, I realised, as I was now running out of the essentials, I was free to go shopping and get some.

He was to be cremated. We'd talked about it when he was alive. When my Granddad died, he, like me, preferred that idea. Stewart's ashes were going to be laid to rest at Margate's St John's cemetery in their crematorium garden of rest, which for me was nice as it meant I could easily go and visit him.

So, after another cry and another cup of tea, I let Mark know what was happening and then went shopping at Aldi.

I walked, didn't fancy riding, but I went the route we would have ridden and it was nice. The weather held off and it was a pleasant walk.

I had a cup of tea at M&S, no Eccles cakes but there was an apple turnover so I had that, found a table by the window and sat on my normal side, able to look over to Sheppey in the distance. Then I went to Aldi to buy a newspaper, milk and bread. It was quiet there and it took me no time to do my shopping. Then I headed back, relaxed reading the paper and then started thinking about a suit for the funeral, looking up the prices as well as for wreaths online, before having something to eat.

For the first time in three years, there wasn't too much mash.

I was about to settle down to watch a movie when Mark rang and we had a couple of minutes' chat. He wanted to make sure I was alright and in the course of the conversation I mentioned that I didn't have a picture of Stewart.

I had had one on my old phone, one with him sitting on the then new leather sofa with Jason the cat, who was at that time just a kitten, and the picture was taken originally for Stewart of the cat, but it had been the only picture I had. Well, I saw him every day by then, so what did I need a picture for? But I'd accidently dropped the phone and although I'm sure for a price someone could have got that and other images off it for me, I hadn't bothered. I'd just replaced the phone with a smart one.

But Mark said he had a picture, taken when Stewart had come to his flat around 2013-14, and he said he was smiling in it and that I could have it if I wanted it. He said he also thought he had some others from when they used to visit the Umbrella Centre, around the 2003-2004. He said if he could find them, he'd bring them too when we met up next.

Wasn't sure when that would be but it was reassuring that I hadn't lost him twice.

26

The next day I planned to be just busy around the flat. I had a lot to do and so went on and did it.

About half two, when I was almost finished and my thoughts were turning to having something to eat, Graham called me. They still hadn't found a home for the cat but were thinking of trying the RSPCA.

The main reason for the call was to tell me about the funeral arrangements. It was going to be at Margate Crematorium at 13.45 on 30 August. He was hoping to take Mark and me down in the car but until he'd had enough time to talk to the other family members who wanted to come, he wasn't sure if he'd have room, so Mark and I could still have to go by train. If he did have room, we were going to meet the hearse at the undertaker's and follow it to the crematorium. However, he said he'd confirm everything in writing on Monday when he would come and see me.

He also asked me what music would Stewart have liked for the funeral.

Because of his love of fishing, even though he hadn't done it for fifteen years at least but still had some of his rods in the attic and had been thinking of doing it again now he had his picnic basket, the family had chosen 'Gone Fishing' by Bing Crosby to play on the way out.

So I began to think about what tunes he had had on his MP3, in his CD collection and then after a cup of tea and a little thought, I realised that this was the wrong approach. I started to think about the little feller again, about when we were hanging together and what he sort of hummed and sang.

Now I tend to have about two dozen songs I sing to myself if stressed or doing something boring around the house or cycling on an empty road, the sort of places or activities where a bit of music would be nice but for obvious reasons having your head in earphones wouldn't be a good idea.

And these are the sorts of songs I would listen to, till eternity and so applying the same logic to my friend, I began to recall his favourite tunes.

He was always talking about Queen, as I think he most admired Freddie Mercury's audacity as a performer as well as Brian's May's guitar skills, and George Michael, though he seemed to be always singing Wham songs so I probably should say Andrew Ridgley as well.

When George died, he'd gone out and bought the album of his greatest hits that was released in tribute. He hadn't done the same for Prince or David Bowie so George had to be a favourite and, unlike a lot of the CDs he had, once bought they had ended up on a shelf, probably never played. He had kept this one on the table and played it more than once.

All I had to do now was come up with a list of songs from both artists, probably in favourite order and let the family make the final choice. Well, whichever, that would wait until Monday as the next two days I was going to be left to my own devices. Saturday I was usually in during the daytime to do my housework but Sunday was going to be the big test, my first Sunday dinner in thirteen years, other than when I was visiting people, which I wasn't going to be sharing with Stewart.

On the radio, about the time I was going to bed, they had an 80s programme and I decided to put to the clock radio on sleeper mode, let it play and listen to the programme as I expected at some point a song by one of those artists would come on. In particular I wanted to hear George Michael or Wham, as Queen, at first, I thought would be easy to figure out.

The only tunes I knew we shouldn't use were Bad Boys and Wake Me Up Before You Go Go, not because you can't have jolly songs at a funeral. They are after all supposed to reflect the person not the occasion. However, he being one of those sensitive kinds of people, it would be fairer to say George's ballads were more his thing.

For the first half hour, no joy. Prince got a look in but nothing of the two artists that mattered. It looked like the timer was going to run out and I was going to have to just choose, as the DJ kept going on about her guest later in the show and I was getting so tired, when came the montage year.

This was where she played a snippet of the songs, five up to two, this week on a given year, and then played all the way through what had been number one. So I listened and discovered number one nearly thirty years ago on the same week on which my best friend died was George Michael, 'Careless Whisper.'

So 'Careless Whisper' was going to be one of my suggestions.

27

Saturday began as a normal day, though after the usual domestic chores, I was going to put the cookery books away and put out all my adventure and crime novels instead. As good as these cookbooks were, it's hard to get enthused about making anything or putting a menu together if you're doing it for one, and some of the recipes, the ones we had done regularly over the past four years, I already knew off by heart. So they were being packed away until there was someone else to cook for.

I was also going to have to tune in a radio for the football results as I'd become so used to knowing them, it was going to seem strange not to.

My thoughts turned to Queen and the second song for Stewart. I like Queen, but I'm not a fan. That is to say, I like hearing their music, even have an album, but I would never have gone to a gig unless Stewart had wanted to see them and had asked me to come along. But thinking about their music, I realised there was a lot of it to choose from.

Now, Stewart was never able to really express himself easily. The condition made it hard for him to do so. If he said he liked something or it was good, it meant he really loved it and the thing was brilliant. Normally, in the world of a person without his condition, that 'good' would be replaced by two, three or more paragraphs of conversation. For most of us, that 'good' would enable us to talk about that thing with so much passion that, to those around us who weren't interested, we'd seem like right know-it-all bores, to our friends and family either a bit of a geek or an anorak, and to those who were either in the loop or mildly interested, knowledgeable and well informed.

So 'good' meant a lot, 'really good' meant even more, and 'brilliant' meant it was unsurpassed, but you could never get any more depth from him than that without it being a struggle.

When we'd watched a film together, if he had really liked it, like Tremors for example, he'd say to me as the film finished, 'That was really good, wasn't it?' meaning he had really enjoyed it and was hoping I had too.

I'd agree it's a good fun movie, no denying that, and would be a welcome addition to any film fan's collection but to make more of an evening of it I'd ask him what he liked about it.

He'd say, 'The Worms.'

I'd say how I liked the way the director and writer treated us the audience as intelligent, knowing that we knew already all the monster horror conventions and, within the limitations of the creatures themselves, made them both smart, as smart as our heroes, along with creating several interesting and different characters, all of whom you cared about. I'd also say how Kevin Bacon and Finn Carter were obviously destined to become the love interests but, as the whole relationship doesn't start until after the film is effectively over, it is really padding out the last three minutes to help wind us down emotionally and make a plot device ready for a sequel.

If I was with another film buff, we would talk about the camera work, the choice of casting, the plot, that sort of thing and probably could have spent over an hour talking about the film and that's just a fun little popcorn filler.

So you realise the problem I had thinking about which Queen song he liked best, as when we'd see one of the Top of the Pops repeats or a performance in a documentary about the band, it was always, 'they were a good band', 'brilliant', 'wasn't he good.'

So pinning it down to a couple of choices was hard, especially as listening to Queen songs to get an idea only set me off all teary again, so before I tackled the tidying up of my flat, I texted by brother Paul, a lifelong Queen fan, and asked him to choose a song that any dedicated fan would like at their funeral.

He replied he would have a think and get back. I expected that he'd be doing that during work so I got on with the rest of my day in the certain knowledge that the right song would be suggested.

I didn't in the end do all my housework. It was a nice sunny day so I went for a walk as it turned out, around Whitstable thinking of Stewart and his music.

28

On Sunday, I started thinking about the funeral, which in turn started me thinking about what Graham had said about what the corner had told him. Now I'd always assumed if you'd suffocated or had a heart attack caused by a blocked artery or something, then the post-mortem would have detected this, but from what Graham had said, no one else or even Stewart himself had killed him and, as far as the natural cause of death was concerned, there was nothing about his general health to indicate how he died.

Which sort of suggested it wasn't a blocked artery or him knocking his head in a fall or anything like that. But not being a doctor, all I could do was speculate though I was now puzzled and bemused by it all.

Despite some ups and down, the past four years he'd had more ups, to a point where he wasn't recognisable as the man he'd been even before the dark days.

Mark had noticed, saying about the last two years 'He was at his fittest, on an upswing, happy, lucid, talkative, everything we knew he was. This was him at his best.'

He was happy, adventurous, making plans for the future, even to the point where we were talking of getting him a passport and doing a bit of wine shopping in France for Christmas and, as I needed to renew mine, we were going to do that together, at the end of September to get them in time for the Christmas markets.

Stewart had been cycling regularly for the last three years, of course, with the subtle diet changes. Mark had only noticed the changes in the last two years but he was essentially right. In the last four years Stewart had been happy, bright, and intelligent and could hold an intelligent conversation on even history or science subjects.

Though his agoraphobia had prevented us going to see Arsenal play, he was finding smaller crowds tolerable if in my company and a daytime screening of a film he wanted to see, once the kids had gone back to school, was also a planned trip. The only thing we hadn't yet decided to do was whether to cycle to Herne Bay or bus it.

Crowds were always going to be the problem but otherwise he had made huge transformations to his life and it had only been getting better for him. If he had had a medical complaint, such as a blocked artery, surely he would have had some signs before then, signs which even I could have noticed.

I looked up the signs for heart attack, and apart from the fatigue, any of the other signs were also consistent with schizophrenia, which meant he'd had a heart attack every day for the past twenty years, if I took these symptoms as a warning sign, so, unless the coroner had missed the obvious, he had no real issues there.

I had dinner, having some wine with it, like we would normally have had. Then I sat down to watch a bit of telly and had a quiet afternoon.

Paul had got back to me by now and the number one Queen song on the list was Teo Torriatte, from the Album 'A Day at the Races'.

Actually, after a while of thinking about the funeral itself, I knew I understood Stewart's mind better than most people, having spent the most time with him, and I began to think about how he would have liked the service.

The best way to approach it was to think of it as a conversation with Stewart.

'Forget about the occasion. That's not what it's about. A funeral is about celebrating the life now gone and as it's your day as it were, just like a wedding, you get to choose the music you like or would like to hear rather, if you were there.'

Though I had tried to dismiss it to start with, I could feel him getting more and more uncomfortable at the prospect of the more traditional funeral. Graham had mentioned about readings and hymns, even though he knew Stew wasn't at all religious. He wasn't a humanist or anything. If he was anything, he was probably agnostic, or at least couldn't care less, and I couldn't imagine him choosing any hymns himself.

I decided I was going to ask Graham when I gave him the list, if possible, to drop the hymns and play Teo Torriatte or any of the songs either side of the eulogy all the way through, to replace the hymns with the full songs and we could all just sit there and think of Stewart and enjoy the songs with him.

So I was resolved. I just needed to talk this through with Graham and hope I'd done my best for my best friend.

29

Monday 21 August, one week now since his death, and the first day since the tragedy that is a normal day, in as much as I've no tasks to do for Graham as I've written down the song list, I've no shopping to do until Tuesday and, apart from waiting for the washing machine, all I've got to do is my work.

Strangely enough, instead of waking at 04:30 as I have been doing recently, I'm waking at a more normal time, which means if I worked as normal, I'd be finished at 13:00, or half past if I took a lunch break and would be ready for Stewart to either call round just before 14:00, or ring me to come round to him. Though, of course, today he's not coming whatever and I know it's going to be around noon onwards when the day will start to seem weird again.

Because it's a Monday and I'm in the normal routine, it feels easy at the moment. It's when the routine breaks, that's the next step I've got to survive.

On reflection over the last week, most of it's been a daze, no one moment of it's been too routine, other than trying to eat at the same times, including on Sunday, although I ended up eating two hours earlier. I had been up two hours earlier so in effect the day got shifted by two hours, as after the first 48 hours after I discovered him, there in the bathroom, I'd been going to bed much earlier, my day now started at 3am, but I was at last getting my normal amount of sleep. Saturday had turned out the worst because normally he would have rung me a couple of times and then come round for a coffee but instead I was thinking about songs for his funeral.

But also, I couldn't get on with the normal things I would have done. I would have cleaned the bikes, neither of which I've been able to touch since and no substitute for a good friend.

A week on and there are still moments that make me want to cry as I can't seem to come to terms with the injustice of it all. However, it's the good times I keep remembering, which is probably why it's so upsetting. If he had been so depressed and life had held no joy for him, you could say he was better off but now it's a bit like buying a long novel and just as you're about to find out the answers and resolve the whole plot, the last few pages are missing.

I've had to put a couple of projects on hold, which is a little annoying because I was close to either completing them or getting them into production but, to be honest, at the moment I can't concentrate on them properly so they'll have to wait. I've decided they can wait until after the holiday as I've arranged to see my parents after the funeral. I'll get back to the projects when I can concentrate and so work as it is at the moment is more like treading water, reading over things but not really doing anything new.

However, I kept busy all day and by the time I would normally stop and go to Stewart's, I stopped and just had a cup of tea. I was a bit reflective, but over the worst. Then an hour later, Graham came round to pick up the song ideas for the service and give me my confirmation of the details. That's when I asked him if we could to drop the hymns and play the music in full instead. He said leave it with him and he would see what he could do but there were other family members who wanted an input too.

After that I had something to eat and waited for Mark to ring. His timing was perfect as I'd just washed up and we arranged where to meet on Wednesday. After that I settled down for the night.

I watched a couple of comedy films but basically went to bed early. At the moment, away from the computer, I feel a bit lost, a bit redundant, and on it I don't seem to have the enthusiasm anymore.

In short, I'm in limbo.

30

Tuesday 22nd was simple. I had a list of things to do, and basically all I had to do was stick to it.

I had to go to Aldi first to get some food and bits, then to town to get a haircut and then to Canterbury to get a suit. I had thought about the old suit from 2008, which had lasted through to 2012, my last funeral to date, but too many football matches and too much Sunday dinner wine had meant it was a little tight. I could still wear it but I'd become a bit constipated since his death, the body in shock I think, and I knew if it was a hot day and hot at the ceremony, then I would feel uncomfortable and anyway, I wanted to see Stewart off in style so I was determined to buy a new suit.

So I made a day of it and took the time to have a little look around the city.

It had changed a lot in less than a year, as too had Whitstable since Aldi had opened. I'd only been down twice but in both towns it seemed anything that had closed thanks to the hike in rates was being replaced by restaurants and cocktail bars.

No wonder diabetes, obesity and so forth was on the rise. It's probably been happening for years but only when you're away from somewhere for a while can you see the changes, the same way really that Mark had noticed the changes in Stewart more than I had as I'd seen him change very, very slightly every day. Now, in Whitstable I could see how three new food outlets had opened and two shop areas were being refurbished, not counting the three new cafes that opened last year, and Canterbury was changing in just the same way.

My day started at Aldi at the time of day we would have normally gone but I walked rather than rode and didn't go for a cup of tea, so was in Aldi at the usual time. It was as quiet as normal and, only needing a basket to pick up what I wanted, I was in and out and home in less time than normal.

On the way out, I had glanced down to Stewart's flat and saw the full skip outside. I knew it was largely the furniture, well worn out. The plan had been to start replacing it this year anyway so it didn't surprise me the skip was full. They were all big items but it did for a short moment bring home again why we weren't on our way, riding our 'Beastie Boys' to the shops.

Still couldn't take the short route.

It wasn't just passing his flat and rekindling the memories that I was afraid of but, for the past five or six years, as I had begun to visit every day and as we started cooking together, other people on the estate had come to know me as always visiting Stewart.

It had got to such a point that, whichever way I went or if I was on my way to see him or heading home, or even heading past to go to the Co-op, if I ran into someone who knew Stewart from the bus stop or a neighbour or a fair-weather friend, the first thing they would say was, 'Seen Stewart?' or 'How's Stewie?'. Even if I was heading to his and it was obvious I hadn't seen him yet, always the same question.

Because we were cycling everywhere together then, we'd come to be seen as inseparable and the idea of a load of people either asking about him or saying how sorry they were about his passing was a bit more than I could cope with at that time.

I'd already had that shock once, when I went to get a cup of tea and the cake at M&S that first time and the woman serving me had said, in all innocence,

'On your own today?'

I know she meant nothing by it. After all, since the food hall had been open, it had always been the two of us there at eight in the morning for a tea and cake before we went shopping, the same days, three times a month, so I could see why it was strange at first for her to see me on my own.

But it still hurt, like a sharp knife into the heart.

So, after a cup of tea, I walked to Whitstable to get my haircut, not for any other reason than it being such a nice day I fancied the walk and it gave me time to think.

Was going to go to my normal barber's but I usually only use them because the shop's on the same side of the street, next to the road down which I lock up my bike, and as all the barbershops are the same price and as good as one another, where you go is immaterial really.

So I went to have my haircut at the place where Stewart had his cut, which was a good choice as almost as soon as I sat down a barber was free and I was out of there quicker than expected. So, just after midday, I went to the library stop to catch the bus.

Now here's how stupid the world is. At first, I asked for a return, which would have been one way to the city and then as far back into Whitstable as the library, but a roaming ticket would give me unlimited journeys until 11 o'clock at night, anywhere around most of Kent to East Sussex, so I could have gone to Herne Bay, Margate, Ashford, Dymchurch and even Royal Tunbridge Wells, all for less than a Whitstable to Canterbury return.

It was £1 cheaper for the roaming ticket.

Three years before, when I had last bought a return ticket, the return was just ten pence cheaper than the roaming ticket. Now the roaming ticket was cheaper and I could pass that ticket on or I could have made another journey.

Think it's about time this country invested in education.

Even buying the suit turned out to be a bit depressing because in the days when I last went to a proper clothes store and bought a suit, you had suited staff, who attended to you from almost the moment you first walked in, in such a way that you felt a little intimidated but also a bit flattered and a bit special.

Now it was just find the stuff yourself as the staff go hide. Also, suits now don't come complete on the peg. You can buy them complete but each element is on a separate rail. Anyhow, it's not until you are at the point of actually buying it, do you get the advice from a member of staff, who's dressed so casually that he or she needs an identity tag to show that they're actually staff.

Not saying they weren't helpful or didn't do a good job, it's just looking for the person wearing the conference tag round his neck and being ignored for most the time I was there actually looking wasn't the fun experience it had once been before shopping became a leisure activity.

Headed home as planned, getting off the bus at Clapham Hill. The bus continued to Estuary View so I could have got off another stop later but I wanted to walk down the old Thanet Way and was home by half two.

I put the suit away until Saturday when I would make sure it wasn't creased and would polish my shoes and have everything ready. Then I had a light dinner with some of the salad I'd bought earlier, watched a DVD, then called it an early night.

Tomorrow I was going to get some counselling advice, meet up with Mark and sort out the floral tribute. I was going to use a line from one of my books that Stewart read and loved.

He was reading it for the second time when all this happened and it seemed a fitting tribute.

31

Wednesday.

Bereavement counselling.

The doctor asked me six questions which I answered truthfully. The conclusion: I was suffering from grief, should take some time off work, but didn't need any anti-depressants and if I wanted I could have some sleeping pills. With a bit of time and a bit of rest it would pass, then my energy would come back and I would be able to continue anew.

He even agreed I should take a couple of weeks off and spend them with my folks in Wales to let the grief come out. It was a natural process and it would lessen in time.

Good words and I declined the sleeping pills. I knew once Stewart was laid to rest, I would start to get the sleep I needed.

I booked the ticket to leave one week after the funeral, allowing time for the tickets to arrive by post and booking a quiet coach each way. Was thinking of first class as it's not much dearer except at Christmas but might treat myself to that come Christmas instead.

I was going to be sort out the flowers later after meeting Mark in the afternoon and then I was going to spend the next couple of days doing those odd jobs put off because of work. Work was going to slide into a three-month delay now but it didn't matter. It would always be there so what was the worry?

I read the sheet Graham gave me.

'Funeral arrangements for Stewart. Stewart is to be cremated at Thanet Crematorium, Manston Road, Margate CT9 4LY. Date 30th August 2017, time 13:45. Flowers may be sent to the undertakers,'

A nice touch I thought, as he liked flowers, liked gardens and nature.

'to be there by 11am on the morning of the funeral. Gore Brothers, 56-60 Thanet Road, Margate, CT9 1UB. If you wish to follow the hearse, you must be at the undertakers by 13:00 hrs. After the funeral, we shall be going to the Labour Club in Whitstable. 12 Belmont Road, Whitstable, CT5 1QP.'

I took the details with me and wrote out the message I wanted to send with the display.

'My best friend, "we all have worth, we all have love inside us", Tony'.

I wanted to use the quote from 'Waiting for a Train'.

It was one of three books of mine he'd read but the only one with anything quotable you could use at a funeral. Knowing he liked the books, the long books and the short books I'd written, and had been pestering me to write a couple more for him, I knew he'd have appreciated the quote.

I met Mark as arranged but not in the coffee shop we planned. It was too busy and, it being small, we would have had to sit outside and we didn't want to have to compete with the traffic so we went to the cafe next door but one, The Burgate.

It was nice and quiet in there because it's more London prices than Whitstable but we were able to make our arrangements and Mark decided there and then to come with me to choose his flowers too.

So we went to the last floral shop in town which hadn't been converted into a cafe, a nail bar or a vegan restaurant and had a look at their display books.

Looking at them and dismissing the simple posy type, I considered the wild flower displays but the best one included apples, was a bit out of my budget and also was quite large and I didn't want to buy anything that would upstage whatever the family bought to go on top of the coffin.

I wanted something that could travel by the side of the coffin and I settled for a wreath, one with red roses so that with the white carnations it would look more like his beloved Arsenal's colours.

Again, I thought he'd like that touch.

I handed over the message and they copied down the details. Then Mark chose his wreath and wrote a message and that was that for the day.

Only then I realised I hadn't eaten and it was two hours past my usual dinner time so when I got home, I was starving but happy now that the floral tribute was sorted. I wasn't showing symptoms of being overly depressed or anything and now had only to get all my stuff ready for the big day, which I was still planning to do on Saturday, and so for the next couple of days threw myself into sorting out some generally neglected household chores.

I was going to take time off until 20 September what with the holiday and all.

The next four weeks were going to be simple and hopefully by the end of them, I'd know why he died as the coroner's report should be in I hoped. Then it would all be at an end and I would be able to move on, refreshed, to continue with all the vim and vigour I would need to both get the next book out and my other projects back on track.

32

Thursday and Friday were unusual because they were so unremarkable. Thursday I spent what turned out to be the whole day sorting out rubbish to take to the recycle centre and baking some bread in my bread maker.

The only remarkable thing about that day was I actually got it all done whilst listening to the radio.

Friday I was going to have to shop first thing in the morning and was thinking, now that I didn't need to buy so much or carry so much as I was only getting my own, of getting a cheap second-hand mountain bike for shopping and general stuff around town and keeping the 'Beastie Boy' for leisure riding and any big shopping trips, like Christmas food, drink, that sort of thing, as then I might need a rack.

I was toying with the idea of getting some panniers like Stewart had, but as most of my shopping would fit neatly with a bit of space into a single rucksack, if on the odd occasion I did need to buy more, then the rack alone would be enough. If anything changed, I could get some later. I knew the type he'd had so knew they'd be easy to find again on Amazon.

On Friday I was going to try and meet up with Stewart's other friend, the one he liked to see every now and then, Robert, and give him the sad news.

I was going to have to catch him as I'd not seen Stewart's red notebook since the police had it and, though I'd mentioned it to Graham, I think if it had been found, it was probably binned as it did look scruffy. Not knowing the book's fate, the only chance I had to give Robert the opportunity to pay his respects was to catch him on a day I sort of knew he was likely to be at home.

He was a creature of habit so everything was in my favour. I was just hoping he hadn't taken this week to go off and visit his relatives back home in his native Cornwall.

Shopping went well. I walked but again it was a nice sunny day. The only disappointment, or rather an irony, was that Aldi had just introduced a brand new line of bread mixes for bread makers, something Stewart had wished to try, wanting to get his old machine out and to get into making his own bread again for the weekends. However, at the Co-op he couldn't find where they kept it and anyway it was dearer there than top-priced loaf. Here at Aldi, it was cheaper than a loaf, other than the economy bread, so worth buying, just a shame they were a week too late.

I was set now until Tuesday, when I would need to get some more milk, as I was no longer buying the four-pint bottles because I had only really had so much milk for when Stewart would come round as he liked his tea very milky, like the French drink it. So at least the day before the funeral I was going to keep myself busy with the shopping and things and not get morbid before the day itself.

I planned to go to town around one to try and catch Robert. Otherwise, if I was around the bowling alley area at the time we'd normally be finished, about twenty past three, I'd catch him coming back home so I wrote out the details for him then started to think what to do with the day.

I'd just put the coffee machine on when Graham rang, telling me that firstly the cat was now in a good home, Dan had found someone, which was a relief, and secondly that there would be seven of us, including Mark and me, in the limo to follow the coffin but one of us would have to sit up front.

The Goth in me without hesitation wanted to be up front. Ideally I would have liked to have ridden in the hearse with the coffin but up front with the limo driver seemed the best compromise so I offered to save the hassle of everyone trying to defer it to someone else and volunteered.

Be a bit like old times on the bike. When we were coming back from our picnic, he'd lead the way then, I would lead going shopping or bowling, and I had a wry smile about that for the next hour or so as I imagined the two of us heading to his favourite spot to have our sandwiches.

I was considering going shopping again to get some salad and do just that on the Bank Holiday but thought about the Lycra brigade and the extra traffic. The year before when I'd just got my 'Beastie Boy', we'd gone there on a Bank Holiday and, though the picnic had been nice, the cars and road bikes constantly streaming by made it a fraught journey, the sort where, instead of enjoying the sun, sea, air and glancing over the marshes or the estuary and thinking isn't it wonderful to be busy doing nothing, we'd be forever glancing in our rear mirrors, negotiating round the parked cars and not really having a chance to ride side by side and chat.

So I decided on Tuesday's shop. I was going to shop big, as it were, and not just get what I needed for the week but get some stuff for a picnic too. I had my own lunchbox I could use and I'd go to his favourite spot and have our last picnic there, after the funeral, as my own personal, last, fond farewell.

I actually set off at two and went straight to Rob's address. It wasn't too hard to find, although it wasn't straightforward either, and luckily Rob was running late and I caught him in.

I told him the bad news, saw the red rings around the eyes and could see he was a little shocked and upset. I spent half an hour with him, chatting and going through the details.

I had to apologise for not getting in touch sooner but, as I explained to him, it had taken me the week to get myself back together before I could think about anything else.

We agreed to hook up the next time I went bowling and I hoped to see him at the funeral.

He was going to tell Ronnie later that afternoon as well as another friend I didn't really know but who knew Stewart well in those years before he moved to Seasalter and had kept in touch. So I left and headed home for a quiet night in.

It was also a therapeutic Saturday for me, largely a day of polishing things.

I had my shoes to polish, getting them all nice and shiny for the occasion, but I also cleaned and polished my 'Beastie Boy' ready to ride it again after the funeral for my last shopping trip before I headed away. Only it seemed right to keep it off the road until then, out of respect for those days we'd ridden to the shops, the picnics and town together.

Sunday was just dinner as usual and a couple of movies.

Monday was check the suit had no creases, the shirt was ironed and the black tie wasn't twisted. Around half one in the afternoon, Graham rang to confirm they were going to pick us up from Dan's place and we had to be there by twelve.

I texted this to Mark and knew he'd go through it again on Tuesday.

My suit was ready, I was mentally prepared and, apart from a bit of shopping to do Tuesday morning, there wasn't much more to think about.

Mark rang me back and agreed to ring again on Tuesday. We arranged that I was going to be picked up by Chris, a friend of his, and he would drop us off at Dan's before we'd be picked up by the family and taken to the undertaker's.

33

Wednesday, 30 August 2017.

I woke early from a fitful night.

I had laid out the suit and everything ready the night before and had decided to have a salad brunch around ten so that I wouldn't feel hungry or faint during the funeral. It was important to keep the blood sugar level up. The funeral was going to be stressful enough without having to fight off hunger too.

At eleven I would get ready and by quarter to twelve Mark would arrive with his friend Chris to drop us off at Dan's for midday.

According to the advance weather forecast, it was supposed to be dry. However, on the day, it was showers with rain later.

Why is it never sunny for a funeral?

But even that turned out to be inaccurate as, by the time I had finished getting ready and was all suited up waiting for Mark, we had a raging monsoon lashing at the window.

Mark arrived duly early as Chris liked to plan for any eventuality which turned out to be wise planning indeed, considering the weather and Wednesday being the day they decided to dig up and block off a large section of Joy Lane, meaning we had a small detour to take.

Almost soaked through just from going a few yards from car to door, we were soon at Dan's and waiting for Sue and Graham to arrive. I noticed Dan had Stewart's bike in his living room, which I hope he keeps as I was wondering what had happened to it as I'd polished mine. It looked good in his house and a bit cleaner. I suspect Dan had run a cloth over it and I didn't notice the flag on the back but in a way it was fitting that flag no longer flew on the back.

They were due to pick us up at 12:30 but arrived about quarter past and we headed off almost immediately, which again turned out to be a smart move as the heavy rain was making driving through town horrendous as the drowning roads and the slow traffic bunched up made the town almost grind to gridlock but, using a couple of the back roads, we got onto the motorway and were heading for Birchington in good time.

Birchington was the part of the journey I was dreading as it was August, the height of the tourist season, and a village that has basically one road leading through it and into a small pinch point with all the village roads converging into the centre of the old market green or, as it is now, the roundabout by the church surrounded by shops. It was here, as we came off the dual carriageway and headed up the hill into Birchington, that I was expecting what would normally happen, hitting a traffic queue and spending five minutes crawling through there before a second dual carriageway whisked us through to Garlinge and down into Margate where the next area of concern would arise after passing where the old Sea Bathing Hospital used to be and the amusements along the 'Golden Mile'.

So I was ready in my mind to suggest heading out to Quex Park and following Shottendane Road but because of the rain we were running a bit close to time. Luckily, there wasn't much traffic apart from the odd works van and taxi at Birchington. It was more like 1am than nearer 1pm and we sailed on through and were past St Ursuline College and into Westgate in less time than we anticipated and, as we passed the next get-out-of-trouble road, George the Fifth Avenue, and approached the steep bridge to the outer edges of Margate town and the dreaded 'Golden Mile', there was hardly a car moving anywhere, and we were soon on the seafront.

The arcades were open but the big wheel and the amusement park itself were closed, at least for the next few hours, as the rain lashing down and the strong wind would have made it impossible to do anything there but eat candy floss out of a bag. The beach, normally packed deep with sun worshippers like sardines, was empty. There wasn't even the usual brave fool in shorts going for a walk come what may, as the brown-turquoise waves crashed down on the flat golden sands.

Graham was using the satnav to get us to the undertaker's, taking us to Thanet Road via Cecil Square. Some of the family were already there waiting and, although as you would expect everyone was anxious to get things going, there was a general quiet calm amongst us and so by half one, we were on our way.

All our flowers were there. His parents had bought the large display on the coffin and an Arsenal scarf they'd bought specially for the day, draped over the foot end, which was to be cremated with him.

As we made our way to the limo, I noticed a red-and-white wreath was resting against the coffin and saw my card, halfway along, on the passenger's side of the hearse. Not only would I be able to watch the coffin but I would be in line with my wreath all the way and from that moment on, I felt it was going to be a good day.

As agreed, I was in the front with the driver, watching the coffin as we followed the hearse. The rain was easing now, light as the forecast had indicated. There was definitely a streak of blue in the sky and it was getting brighter. The cars were facing away from the park, and so we headed back along Thanet Road, towards Cecil Square.

The procession headed across the square, passing the library, the shopping arcade and across the High Street, probably not intentional but fitting, reminding me of the time we'd taken those bikes to Halfords as, after our burgers, we'd alighted at Cecil Square before exploring the town. Stewart had bought his pet stuff and those earphones in the High Street we passed and we'd walked down the other half of the High Street to the harbour for a coffee.

We came down the hill at Marine Terrace, the road we almost reached the bottom of when we were going to visit Dreamland before anxiety got the better of him and we had gone back to get our bus home. We cruised the 'Golden Mile', passing the arcades, Dreamland and the newly restored cinema and then along until, just before the bridge, we turned left, over another bridge that took us on a long straight road, past All Saints Church, Hartsdown Park, the football ground, Tivoli Park and woodland, on the other side of that park we'd ridden past two years earlier, then up the steep hill to the five-road junction that led past the school and to the cemetery.

Because of the weather, the traffic was light, the following cars were able to keep up with us and we entered the driveway up to the crematorium in one long procession meeting up with those who had gone ahead.

The previous service was just finishing. Jason, the minister overseeing the service, met us in the large waiting room and now with the rest of the extended clan, those who could make it that was, this large room was now looking rather small.

A Queen song began to play and that was our cue to come in to the hall.

His coffin, a light-oak colour with nice shiny brass handles, up on the plinth, looked quite small as we entered. I had though it looked quite small in the hearse but there alone on the plinth, with the Arsenal scarf and the red-and-white floral display stretching out over half the coffin, he seemed even smaller, a little lost even.

Being friends not family, we were at the back but there were four full rows ahead of Mark and me and, although Robert didn't show, Stewart's favourite nephews, Connor and Anthony, were both there, as well as Becky and others he'd mentioned over the years when he had wanted to talk about his family and I'm sure, had he been there, he would have been both bemused by such a turnout and overwhelmed that so many genuinely cared.

Before a word was uttered, some of the family, especially Sue I noticed, were already shedding a tear as Graham had to comfort her throughout.

His love of fishing, his cat Jason, his love of Queen, myself, Mark, other members of the family and ten-pin bowling all got a mention. Jason the minister performed a lovely service, keeping both the reverence of the occasion and the fun Stewart shared with us in his eulogy.

There were no hymns, which was right. To praise God's memory when you're not religious would have been hypocritical and he wouldn't have wanted that. Instead two pop songs, chosen to say farewell to Stewart, were played instead and it was nicer listening to them and thinking of him to really feel at peace with him.

A nice touch he would have been thrilled about and which would have filled him with pride was that between the two songs, Connor read the charming poem 'Death Is Nothing At All', by Henry

Scott Holland. It was very touching and brave of him, not being someone who either seeks the limelight or is accustomed to speaking in public. He read with the occasional pause to wipe away his tears through his emotions at his heartfelt grief.

The Lord's Prayer, the only concession to religion, we all said. Then, as Louis Armstrong and Bing Crosby played us out, we looked at the tributes.

There were eight or nine, mine and Mark's like bookends, the ones on the wall by Stewart's name plate, and with an exception of one bunch of wild flowers, all the rest were red and white, for his team.

I looked at my wreath after looking at the others. It was as good as I had hoped it would be and, after we'd all paid our respects to Sue and Graham, we were back in the limo, as the driver collected the cards and handed them to Graham. While we waited, Graham said he thought Stewart's ashes, which were to be scattered, were going to be on row B in the Rose Garden, the final details he would get back to me on later.

Then we headed off, less those who didn't come down with Graham, taking the shorter route across at the lights, pass the school alleyway Stewart and I had taken those bikes for Africa down, then up the hill towards Draper's Mill before following Dane Park round and back to the undertakers. If we'd gone up to the Hornby Museum and Halfords, we'd have traced Stewart's entire Margate adventure.

Though the rain had been light by the end of the service, it didn't stop completely until we were back at Thanet Road. It even warmed up and became sunny.

Leaving there, we rounded the road past the park's entrance, took Dane Road bringing us out at the foot of the hill that leads into Cliftonville, went across into the old part of Margate coming out at the old harbour, and passed that coffee shop where we'd had a drink and a cake before strolling up the High Street and seeing how far the regeneration had reached before Stewart had taken some money out of the bank.

We swept by the 'Golden Mile' for the last time and before long we were on the old Thanet Way, coming down Millstrood Road and on to the Labour Club and, whilst Graham went to park the car, we all followed Sue inside.

There we chatted to the family, had a few drinks, ate some of the nice sandwiches, cocktail sausages, mini pasties and other bits set out on the buffet, again all the sort of food Stewart would have loved and with his favourite beer too. At half five, as the evening drifted to the few core family members, Mark and I said our goodbyes and went to meet Chris for our lift back home.

34

I didn't sleep at all that night. Every time I tried to, I would think of some happy moment spent with Stewart, the bowling alley, The Peter Cushing, along the seafront, or just at his flat. Something to remember each time, something that made me smile, shake my head in disbelief or occasionally feel a little disappointed these things were never going to happen again.

It meant what I had planned for Thursday didn't happen. I was too exhausted to do much but it didn't become mournful either.

I might not have been out on the bike. Instead, I went back to doing some writing and found it a most relaxing way to spend the day after.

I was, however, determined before the summer season ended to fulfil the last definite plan we had made together and that was a picnic at his favourite spot.

Like normal, I'd have homemade sandwiches, pork pies, Scotch eggs and a beer, though a lot less of them as it was going to be only me. I wasn't sure which day it would be at that moment but if I wasn't too fatigued come Friday, I'd get all the bits together then or Saturday and do it on Monday, after I'd sent my brother's birthday presents off.

I also realised during one of my contemplative moments of the day the reason why I wasn't so teary at the funeral, just quiet and reflective. In the first week, I'd had all the big grief outpouring, as finding him and all that happened that week had overwhelmed me but in the second week, preparing for the funeral, and not having anything else to do other than that, meant I was prepared, more so than most, to say goodbye at the crematorium and others there, who really had been preparing longer but until they saw the coffin hadn't had the same sense of the reality of it all, were then most affected.

Having been in their position at my grandparents' funerals, I recalled neither hit me until the first sight of the coffins and they were both expected deaths after short illnesses, but this time, to see the coffin, even just in the back of the hearse, had been a sight for fond remembrance. With all the tributes around that little box, I could imagine him smiling there. I had suddenly felt all serene inside, still sad that we had to be there, but overwhelmed with inner peace.

Friday was a lovely day but I slept in longer, catching up on the night before, so didn't leave for town as early as I hoped. I was heading into Whitstable for a birthday card, so riding the 'Beastie Boy' for the first time in nearly three weeks was a much longer ride than normal as I was a little out of practice.

However, in town I couldn't find the right card and had to get one from Tesco.

I decided Tuesday, as Monday looked like rain, would be the picnic day and also the perfect day to get my supplies for the train journey as well as post Paul's present so Tuesday would be the next busy day on the bike. Monday would be getting everything ready for my trip, with Wednesday the last day to get things sorted and then off to Wales.

All I had now was a quiet weekend to get over and then get ready for the holiday to get life back in perspective.

*

So, our final picnic at our favourite spot on the morning of Tuesday 5 September. Though it was a cloudy start to the day and it felt like a little very light rain in the air, I set off nice and early to get to Aldi to pick up the picnic supplies.

I decided not to ride. I think in part, it was still a little raw getting on the 'Beastie Boy' and riding it to a place where I had only ridden with Stewart. I was going to have to ride up there again at some point but I decided to wait until I returned from Wales. All I needed to do that day was buy the picnic stuff so I walked.

I left at our usual time but didn't follow the exact route, taking a shortcut past the old church to get to the common, not a route we could have taken before as the cruisers' wide handlebars couldn't pass through the gate as a mountain bike's could.

My old stride had returned I had noticed in the first week after his death. As a result, it took me an extra ten minutes to walk a familiar distance, like to town or back, and I was slower getting to Aldi but this time I was there at the same time we would have got there on our bikes, or rather maybe a couple of minutes later, as we often got there two minutes before they opened.

Admittedly I had a second shortcut, the pedestrian stairs halfway up the Old Thanet Way, so with the church I'd covered a shorter distance but it was weird. For the first time since 14 August, I had arrived at the same time we always arrived.

It felt really strange as I reached the shop front. It felt like I should have locked up the bike and subconsciously I drifted over to the cycle rack by M&S before I decided to treat the day like our normal shopping day and so went in to have a cup of tea and a cake.

No Eccles cakes but there was an apple turnover, so I had that. This one was a bit warmer and crisper, certainly better than the last one we had had together. Maybe he had had something there after all.

I chose our regular table by the window. I sorted out the plates and so on from the tray to my position, then took off my rucksack and hat, sat down and had my tea and cake. Then as I checked my watch, I noticed it had taken from the moment I had entered to the moment I was about to leave exactly the same length of time it would have taken when we were together, twenty minutes.

However, it didn't take nearly as long round Aldi. I was in and out in fourteen minutes and walking back, getting home before nine, the same sort of time we would have returned with the bikes. It felt like a normal shopping day as we'd always done it, only he wasn't there to talk to going or coming back.

That's why it felt so weird. It was as if I was on our normal schedule, okay without the bike and walking back home. I did well up a couple of times but this time no crying. Maybe not riding the bike then was a good idea.

I had everything I needed for the picnic and was going to cycle there on the 'Beastie Boy', though this was going to be weird too, going to a place I'd only ever been to with someone else but this time without them. Now all I need was it to be dry around one o'clock, our usual picnic time.

The plan was to post my brother's present in town, get some supplies to eat on my journey to Wales and then ride up to the picnic spot, have the picnic and then come home. So basically, load up with everything, ride off to Whitstable, then past home and on to our picnic spot and then back home again.

If rain was forecast, I could leave it all until Wednesday but today was more fitting, I felt, as the day had already sort of drifted into a day of last tributes.

The very first time we'd been with Mark, in fact the only time we'd had all been on a picnic, it had been cloudy then. Also, the very last picnic we'd both had together had been a cloudy day, with the feeling of rain in the air, though we were home before it happened.

So the day was perfect, mirroring our first and our last picnics.

I left at twenty past twelve to go to town to post the parcel.

Normally we'd get there at about quarter past one and, well, that's the time I got there, unintentionally. I had expected to get there later but there was so little traffic and the wind was with me most of the way, which as any cyclist knows makes it much easier, so I was there at our usual time.

The last time we were here, there had been a noisy holidaymaker with some appalling taste in music which they just had to play so loud it had spoilt things a bit. Today was like the first time this year, quiet, calm and no hint of loud music. The birds were on the water, a couple of young lads walked by behind me so I only heard them without seeing them, and I had my picnic, thinking of those times we'd been up here.

Only the one 'Beastie Boy' parked up and leant against the sea wall, and only one person now sitting on the bench dedicated to Margret Lodge, overlooking the view. She, like us both, loved looking out towards Sheppey.

You could even see the road bridge, which we couldn't see last time as it had been cloudy, and it seemed to have a halo of sun over it, making it shine. For the first time I noticed just how high over the river that bridge is.

I remembered Stewart talking about fishing over in Faversham, how he'd mentioned he was thinking of buying some rods and taking it up again. He had the food basket, he had the bike, a soup flask, the lights and soon he would have had the indicators. All he had needed was a small windbreak and new rods.

I'd actually seen some at a garden sale on the first day I'd ridden the bike again, heading into Whitstable. Had he been alive, I would have told him and we could have cycled down and got them. I wouldn't have bought them on the off chance as I can't tell the difference between lake, river, and sea fishing kit but he would have known.

About twenty minutes to, I noticed the light rain, very light, not really anything to mention, but the clouds were getting darker so I headed back. It hadn't been as large a picnic but I felt I had fulfilled our final promise, the final adventure we'd had already planned and I felt very much at peace.

I also felt happy on the bike again. I'd been somewhere where we'd both been together regularly. That was our place, on a good day, okay, not the hot summerlike days we'd enjoyed for most of this year and those months last year when we'd been out on the 'Beastie Boys', but it had been a place where only us two went and, because it was our spot and I'd survived, I was sure things would become easier from then on.

I came away with an inner peace and a feeling that on a nice sunny day, or even a cloudy one, I could stop there, could sit there and that feeling of us being close again would return.

In fact, I was a little sad and a bit teary when I got back home. Today had been almost a day of our normal routines and keeping to them would help keep the good memories alive.

Soon I would hear when he'd been scattered and how he died I hoped. Once I knew he'd been scattered, I was planning a trip down to the graveyard. Then I'd visit again in May when I visited the rest of my family with my parents.

Next though, I would be travelling to Wales.

35

I took the train and the journey from Whitstable to London was just like any other train journey, no special carriage but, because of the time of day, no commuters either. However, at Rochester we did manage to pick up four of the most incredible bores, who spent the whole journey talking about some case they were representing at court which they were travelling to London for.

And I don't mean anything such as a criminal case or anything. No, these were property lawyers and it was a point about planning procedure. For that half an hour or so, I could feel my brain-cells dying, each committing seppuku one by one.

Thankfully, I had two cheese and onion puffs with me and could eat one to save myself from following suit.

From Victoria it was a short underground journey to Euston and the next train to Crewe for my connection to Shrewsbury where I'd meet up with my folks.

The trip to Crewe was in the quiet coach, which was quieter than the normal coach but not as quiet as it should have been as there were a couple of people who couldn't leave their phones alone, but it was quiet enough to read a book, eat my other puff and I was relaxed by the time we reached our first stop, Crewe.

From there, it was the slowest part of the journey, the stopping service to Shrewsbury but, apart from watching the countryside go by, another largely uneventful journey and so some eight hours later I was at my parents' home.

Travelling light with one small rucksack, most of the space was taken up with my laptop as I felt the change of scene and the quiet would enable me to write.

Of course, they were pleased to see me and wanted to visit a few places whilst I was there, worried that I might get bored being indoors for a fortnight. It being a typical British September, going for a walk along the Dyke was out as it kept raining, making the route all muddy and I didn't have any wellingtons.

Therefore, the two weeks sort of divided themselves into two separate holidays at once. I'd arrived on the Thursday as it would give me an extra weekend and travelling mid-week was always quieter. For the first few days, it was a quiet stay at home, writing during the day and a bit of TV in the evening, mostly watching catch-up episodes of the new series of The Crystal Maze and reflecting that Stewart would have enjoyed this as much as I was.

But from the Monday and thereafter, it was one day out-and-about, the next day in to write. In a way, this helped as on the writing days, there seemed to be a hunger and an urgency to get something done before we went out. I'm sure partly stimulated by the earlier day out, with the mind rested, it seemed to pour out of me more quickly than usual. That or it could also have been that I wasn't cooking so didn't have to worry about shopping, making dinner, that sort of thing, so could just focus on the work. But either way, the system was working and I caught up a lot of lost ground in that week with the projects I'd been working on.

The out-and-about days were less my usual sort of thing, if I'd been on holiday on my own. We didn't visit any art galleries or castles or historical houses and, being September and bitterly cold, going around stately gardens didn't seem like a good idea either.

Also as this was somewhat sprung on my folks, they'd not had time to look up any places of interest I might have liked to go and see which I hadn't already seen. I hadn't had the time to look anything else up either, as the busy routines that had occupied my days had been largely away from the computer, except to buy the rail tickets, so the days out tended to be to farm outlets or garden centres to get ideas for Christmas as September is the time all the displays were being changed ready for the festive season.

It makes a nice change to while away a few hours looking at things, even things you're never going to buy, like a £1200 barbeque with its own temperature gauge, a rambler's walking pole with built-in compass, or a corkscrew set in a case designed to look like a wine bottle, before having a drink and a cake and heading home again, having spent all that time and travelled all that distance just to buy a rose bush or some Christmas cards.

With that and a couple of walks around the town on the days we didn't go to a garden centre or farm outlet, by the time it was time for me to head back home, I was well rested. My mind was focused again and I felt, once I had got back to my normal routines and finished the work I was catching up on, I would be able to get back to the other projects I had almost started in August.

The journey back was better, although I had to ask a member of staff at Birmingham International which end the silent coach would be, which was just as well as I was queuing at the wrong end, but this time at least on our way in to Euston there weren't as many people addicted to their iPhones and I finished my book.

The run to Whitstable was okay and I was home in plenty of time, had dinner and watched a movie. All I had to do now was wait to find out what the coroner's toxicology report would find as waiting to find out how Stewart died was the only annoying fly in the ointment.

36

Back home it was soon obvious that my next publishing project wouldn't be finished before November and I wouldn't therefore get back to the August projects before the end of that month. It suited me, as September continued the weather was getting warmer and nicer and, knowing that Stewart had been scattered by now, I wanted to visit him. I still didn't expect to hear before the end of October for sure what had caused his death anyway and, until I knew, I had this strong urge to want to stay put. The very idea of going away or being away for a while and possibly not being in for the call from Graham was making me a little anxious.

It was, however, a week or so later when we had a really hot day forecast that I decided to go visit Stewart. It was going to be a Wednesday. I checked the day before

on the web to see where the rose garden was but found it wasn't listed on the map. Ringing the office, I soon knew where to find it and then went, round the long way still, to the Co-op to get a sandwich like the ones Stewart always used to buy and a drink to take with me.

That Wednesday I rode down on the 'Beastie Boy', its last ride for the year, and headed to Whitstable Station.

If I had used the Verso, I could have ridden the whole way. It would have only taken an hour and a half but on the cruiser almost three times longer. Setting off for the ten past ten train and wanting to be home again at dinner time, this was the obvious way and, though it was warm for the time of year, it wasn't a hot day.

I could have gone straight to Margate and cycled from there on a mixture of the route we took to Halfords and that which the funeral procession had taken, but it was such a lovely day, I wanted to cycle there and enjoy the ride, making a day of it. So I got off at Birchington, cycled past Epple Bay and then along the esplanade all the way round to Westgate-on-Sea, where it meets the route the hearse took, past the church, Hartsdown Park and so forth.

Getting the bike onto the train carriage itself was a little bit tricky because of the weight and length. I knew the best bet was to put it in backwards and across the opposite door with the front wheel slightly blocking the aisle towards the seats. Fortunately, there is no switching of sides of the track on that part of the route so I wouldn't be in anyone's way and travelling after ten, on the rear coach, hardly anyone to get in the way of. But the length of the bike also meant I had to stand with it the whole way, to stop it falling over, though it's only a six-minute trip, so no real hardship there.

Getting off again was therefore easy. In the time it took to line the bike up, the doors were ready to open. Then following my route along the front, with hardly a breeze to mention, I headed towards Margate cemetery, the long way round.

For the most part, it was an easy ride as, once on the esplanade, it was all flat and the big tyres of the cruiser bike and that well-sprung and wide saddle absorbed all the ruts in the concrete. I was at the gates to the cemetery in good time.

I cycled through the older more Gothic-looking end of the cemetery, with all the old green, lichen-covered stones, statues of angels and the horse, and creeping ivy everywhere, and into the more modern, clean and neatly maintained cremation area.

Next to the scattering lawn and the new area where there are rows of headstones, there is a roundabout area, with a couple of seats ringed by roses.

Most had been deadheaded but a couple were still in bloom. The ring is broken into five sections with room for another to be added. The space was wide enough to put my bike by the bench and still allow people to pass by on their way to the other area of rest behind the hedgerows.

There were a couple of other people by headstones but with the warm sun, the sound of birds in the trees, no breeze, the quiet, and the odd, almost tame, squirrel darting around, it was a nice place to just sit and think about Stewart.

He was scattered around the roses, not sure which but he was there and it felt calming, knowing his remains were there.

After about twenty minutes, I had the sandwich and drink. I was welling up a bit but no one would have noticed, if they had seen me, as I was wearing my sunglasses, and after half an hour I left him, planning to see him next year.

I quickly visited my family members who are honoured there and then headed back the way I'd come to catch my train home.

On the way back, I noticed how many people seemed to start smiling as they saw me riding towards them. I'm sure it's more the bike than my magnetic personality, as you don't get this on a mountain bike, strangers suddenly saying 'hi' or wishing you 'a nice day', as you pedal slowly by.

I was home by half two and happy that his remains were resting in such a nice spot.

37

A few weeks later, as I was listening to a programme on the radio about cardiopulmonary resuscitation, CPR, and defibrillators, one of the caller's description of a sudden cardiac arrest at a golf course, with the victim's face being covered in blood and the talk of there being so much blood as they performed CPR, got me thinking of how I found Stewart and, having still not heard anything back from Graham about the coroner and the toxicology report I listened intently.

Two things came out from that broadcast. Firstly, that 80% of cardiac arrests are fatal, even if CPR is administered even at the moment of them just happening, so my timing may not have made any difference. Secondly, that it's not uncommon for there to be no early warning symptoms. In other words, underlining condition or not, a cardiac arrest could strike at any time, unlike a heart attack which often manifests itself with symptoms long in advance and is often preceded by many minor attacks over a long period of time.

So when Stewart was saying there was nothing wrong when I thought he had a tooth problem and then, with hindsight after his death, had started to wonder if he had had other problems, he was probably being honest in that he hadn't, at least that he was aware of.

The strange way he would sit is a common trait of his condition, as well as with heart disease, but I had been more concerned about his teeth than his heart anyway, as he never seemed to be out of breath doing simple tasks and I remembered the coroner hadn't mentioned his heart as being the reason for his death.

I wondered if this sudden, out of nowhere, cardiac arrest was what had happened, so I started to research, only to discover something even more terrifying than I could have imagined.

For at least the past 30 years it has been known that people with schizophrenia have higher death rates, particularly from cardiovascular causes, than would be expected on the basis of demographics.

Initially, suspicion focused upon lifestyle factors, such as ubiquitous smoking and poor self-care, and perhaps upon a direct effect of the disease. However, in the 1980s some of the suspicion began to shift to the drugs used to treat the disease, fuelled both by the accumulation of case reports among antipsychotic users of serious ventricular arrhythmias and sudden unexpected deaths, as well as advancing understanding of the electrophysiological properties of these drugs.

Some of the evidence suggested that thioridazine, at one time one of the most commonly used medications for major mental disorders, might pose particularly elevated risk.

Numerous case reports also linked this agent with increased risk of sudden unexpected deaths, leading regulatory authorities to change the labelling of thioridazine to discourage use of this agent, unless other antipsychotics are not efficacious, in 2001.

In 2017 the British Medical Journal stated the findings of a comprehensive and careful investigation appeared to support this view, that for those who treat patients with schizophrenia and other major mental disorders with the use of thioridazine, they should only be occasionally used, primarily for patients who do not respond to the atypical antipsychotics or for whom preparations are required.

Unfortunately, several lines of evidence suggest that the story is not so neat. The literature suggests that all currently available antipsychotics have electrophysiological properties that could increase the risk of sudden cardiac death and has been understood to be so since at least 2001.

Indeed, clusters of sudden deaths have kept some promising

new lines off the market and have delayed the licensing of others.

Some epidemiological studies now provide evidence that several of the typical antipsychotics increase the risk of sudden cardiac death. The present study, an impressive achievement, nevertheless did not have sufficient power to demonstrate in a head-to-head comparison that thioridazine was associated with greater risk than the other specific drugs. Because of the time period of the study, the investigators could not study the effects of the atypical agents that replaced it.

38

I was a bit shocked by this, that my best mate, despite check-ups and having no significant heart problems, otherwise surely it would have been noted in the post-mortem, could have died suddenly without warning by just using the medication he was taking.

So I did some further research.

There is an excess mortality rate. Standardised mortality ratios for all causes of death are 1.7 times higher in men and 1.3 times higher in women, in people with psychiatric illnesses, even after allowing for the effect of suicide. This non-suicide elevated risk holds true for people with schizophrenia, or depression, as well as for those with delirium and dementia.

Two major risk factors for excess mortality in psychiatric patients are medical co-morbidity and treatment with antipsychotic medication. The latter is not necessarily causative, as higher doses might be linked with mortality through a confounding factor such as worse physical health in those with more serious mental health problems, though as Stewart was always getting fitter, lifestyle couldn't be attributed to the cause. Some of the side effects of his medication were weight gain and depression, so his medication could have played a part in him getting diabetes, which without my help he wouldn't have maintained under control.

Compared with the overall excess of non-suicide mortality, the number of deaths that might be attributable to medication is small, but most reports seem to argue that iatrogenic mortality must be taken seriously, with appropriate steps taken towards prevention, which have yet to be realised.

The risk of sudden death for individuals receiving antipsychotic drugs was 2.39 times that for 'non-users', according to a four-year retrospective study of 3474 individuals with schizophrenia in the 1990s. The risk of 'all-cause' death and the risk of 'non-suicide cause' death was increased in users of thioxanthenes and atypical antipsychotics.

Antipsychotic drug treatment is a key component of schizophrenia treatment algorithms recommended by the National Institute of Health and Care Excellence (NICE), The American Psychiatric Association, and the British Society for Psychopharmacology.

The main effect of treatment with antipsychotics is to reduce the so-called 'positive' symptoms, including delusions and hallucinations. There is mixed evidence to support a significant impact of antipsychotic use on negative symptoms of schizophrenia, such as apathy, lack of emotional affect, and lack of interest in social interactions, or on the cognitive symptoms, disordered thinking and reduced ability to plan and execute tasks.

In general, the efficacy of antipsychotic treatment in reducing both positive and negative symptoms appears to increase with increasing severity of baseline symptoms.

Whilst cardiovascular causes are most common, accounting for the majority of the 5% of sudden and unexpected deaths, most cases have no clear explanation on post-mortem examination and 'sudden unexplained deaths' are thought to result from fatal arrhythmias.

Retrospective studies show that people with prolongation of the QTc, the interval measured between Q wave and T wave in the heart's electrical cycle, beyond 500ms are at increased risk of serious arrhythmias such as ventricular tachycardia and torsade de pointes.

This is also known as Long QT Syndrome, a disorder of the heart's electrical activity. It can cause sudden, uncontrollable, dangerous arrhythmias in response to exercise or stress. Arrhythmias are problems with the rate or rhythm of the heartbeat, just what you need when you're prone to anxiety attacks.

Sudden unexplained death in individuals with mental health problems was first described in 1849 and a link with antipsychotic drugs was postulated back in 1960. Recently regulatory authorities in several countries have expressed concerns about a relationship between antipsychotics and the risk of QTc interval prolongation, serious arrhythmias and sudden cardiac death. In about 1 in 10 cases, the torsade is fatal. Most antipsychotics prolong the QTc interval, in overdose of course, but some prolong it even at therapeutic doses.

There is only an approximate relationship between QTc prolongation and risk of sudden death, and the risk related to antipsychotics is thought to increase in people with pre-existing cardiac disease, those taking multiple QT-acting drugs and those taking antipsychotics at high dose for long periods as Stewart was.

Sudden death refers to the unexpected death of a person who has no known acutely life-threatening condition and yet dies of a fatal medical cause. The incidence of sudden death in the population is about 400,000 cases per year in the USA and around 80,000 per year in the UK. Sudden death is heralded by abrupt loss of consciousness within 1 hour of the onset of acute symptoms.

39

On 9 November Graham rang me to tell me the coroner's verdict was in. The good news was he hadn't died of a cardiac arrest. Well, at least that wasn't the prime reason for his death. It was cirrhosis of the liver, thought to have come about because of his diabetes.

However, even that sounded strange in that, although I knew cirrhosis of the liver was one of the diseases that diabetes could cause, it normally showed itself with other symptoms, especially in the chronic stages, such as jaundice, and I'd not seen anything like that in Stewart. Even on that last Sunday he was his normal colour and I thought surely his recent eye test would have picked up any jaundice then.

Checking back on the research in to his medication, I found that it worked on inhibiting certain neurotransmitters. Those affected include dopamine, a compound present in the body as a neurotransmitter and a precursor of other substances including adrenaline, the suppression of which leads to type 2 diabetes, noradrenaline, a hormone which is released by the adrenal medulla and by the sympathetic nerves and functions as a neurotransmitter. It is also used as a drug to raise blood pressure and serotonin, a compound present in blood platelets and serum, which constricts the blood vessels and acts as a neurotransmitter.

Dopamine is the primary neurotransmitter affected by taking antipsychotics. An overactive dopamine system may be one cause of the hallucinations and delusions commonly experienced during psychosis. However, many atypical antipsychotics can cause other potentially harmful side effects such as drowsiness, dizziness, restlessness, weight gain, type-2 diabetes, mellitus, hyperlipidemia, which is an umbrella term referring to any of several acquired or genetic disorders that result in a high level of lipids (fats, cholesterol and triglycerides) circulating in the blood as well as QTc interval prolongation, myocarditis, extrapyramidal side effects and cataract, dry mouth, constipation, nausea, vomiting, the last three of which I knew he suffered with, on and off, over all the time I knew him.

Liver failure or hepatic insufficiency is the inability of the liver to perform its normal synthetic and metabolic function as part of normal physiology. Two forms are recognised, acute and chronic.

Acute liver failure is a rapidly developing medical emergency. The condition is also referred to as fulminant hepatic failure, acute hepatic necrosis, fulminant hepatic necrosis and fulminant hepatitis. It occurs when cells of the liver are injured so quickly that the organ cannot repair itself fast enough.

Chronic liver disease in the clinical context is a disease of the liver that involves a process of progressive destruction and regeneration of the liver parenchyma leading to fibrosis and cirrhosis. 'Chronic liver disease' refers to disease of the liver, lasting over a period of six months and consisting of a wide range of liver pathologies including inflammation, liver cirrhosis and hepatocellular carcinoma.

Cirrhosis is a condition where normal liver tissue is replaced by scar tissue (fibrosis). The 'scarring' tends to be a gradual process. The scar tissue affects the normal structure and re-growth of liver cells. Liver cells become damaged and die as scar tissue gradually develops.

Liver failure is a life-threatening condition that requires hospitalization. Many people do not have any liver-damage symptoms until serious liver problems have already developed slowly and silently. Symptoms of end-stage liver disease may include easy bleeding or bruising, persistent or recurring yellowing of the skin and eyes (jaundice), intense itching, loss of appetite, nausea, swelling due to fluid build-up in your abdomen and legs, problems with concentration and memory.

Often associated with alcoholics, non-alcohol liver disease or fatty liver disease and non-alcoholic steatohepatitis are cirrhosis, though it's not clear what causes this type of fatty liver disease. It tends to run in families. It's also more likely to happen to those who are middle-aged and overweight or obese and people that often have high cholesterol and diabetes as well.

The more severe form of NAFLD is called non-alcoholic steatohepatitis (NASH). NASH causes the liver to swell and become damaged. It tends to develop in people who are overweight or obese, or have diabetes, high cholesterol or high triglycerides. Triglycerides are a type of fat found in your blood and high triglycerides might raise your risk of heart disease and may be a sign of metabolic syndrome. Metabolic syndrome is the combination of high blood pressure, high blood sugar, and too much fat around the waist, low HDL ("good") cholesterol, and high triglycerides. Up to 25% of adults with NASH may have cirrhosis.

Even if this had been building up for some time, at least up until the last couple of days Stewart had no obvious symptoms other than appetite loss, but he also had an excessive thirst and was drinking more, suffered tiredness and lack of concentration, which were all symptoms of both diabetes and the side effects of his medication. There was nothing that clearly identified he had any other problem than that caused by his medication or from not taking his pills. If he'd missed them for a few days, due to sleeping during the afternoon, the shakes and the symptoms of the diabetes often resurfaced as much as his mania would a day or two before, which you could argue he'd showed on the Tuesday and Wednesday before he started to get tired.

Antipsychotic drugs, like Risperidone, can damage the liver but this is hidden by the other side effects, which may include weight gain, feeling hot or cold, headache, dizziness, drowsiness, feeling tired, dry mouth, increased appetite, feeling restless or anxious, insomnia, nausea, vomiting, stomach pain, constipation, tremors and a depressed mood.

As for the rest of the top five schizophrenia drugs, the symptoms are broadly the same though Aripiprazole also includes fainting and weakness, mental/mood changes, such as increased anxiety, depression and suicidal thoughts, and trouble swallowing.

Clozapine, also, causes drooling, especially at night, and shaking. Olanzapine also includes pain in your arms or legs, numbness or a tingly feeling, akathisia, which is an inability to sit still, and memory problems. Quetiapine includes dizziness, drowsiness, feeling tired, dry mouth, sore throat, stomach pain, upset stomach, nausea, vomiting and constipation.

As the side effects of the drugs are also the same as those for chronic liver failure, without the jaundice I wasn't so surprised neither of us had spotted it. He'd had a lot of those symptoms for at least fifteen years.

What I also discovered was that the prevalence rate for schizophrenia is approximately 1.1% of the population over the age of 18 or, in other words, at any one time as many as 51 million people worldwide suffer from schizophrenia.

Yet the prevalence of chronic liver disease in patients with schizophrenia (7.0%) was 1.27 times higher than the general population (6.1%) in 2000. The average annual incidence of chronic liver disease in patients with schizophrenia from 2001-2010 was also higher than that of the general population, with younger patients with schizophrenia found to have a much higher prevalence and incidence than those in the general population. Stewart would originally have fallen into this group as he had been on the medication for at least 20 years and diabetes is a significant risk factor for patients with schizophrenia, which is not surprising when type 2 diabetes is an expected side effect of their medication.

So not only are people with schizophrenia, who make up 1% of our population, also more likely to be part of the 6% of our population who suffer with type 2 diabetes, but they are also at higher risk of dying from both cardiac arrest and liver disease as the drugs used immediately put them into a higher-risk category than even recreational drug users, alcoholics or greedy folk.

Knowing that diet is one factor in the onset of diabetes, it staggers me that when Stewart did originally have the carers to look after him, at no time was there any effort made by them to oversee his nutritional needs. Their only concern seemed to be with tidying the flat, paying the bills and making sure he took the medication.

This doesn't just mean because of his medication he was more likely to end up with diabetes but also, because no one helped him to take the steps needed to prevent it, he had no chance of avoiding it.

Expecting Stewart to do it himself despite being aware of the other side effects such as anxiety and loss of concentration, it's no wonder that his condition got worse and he ended up on more medication and at huge expense to the state. These side effects impacted on the sorts of skills he needed to care for himself. To avoid crowds and panic, he bought cheap food in bulk. He couldn't concentrate or work computers well, so when left on his own, he was never going to be able to shop online or follow a recipe book's instructions without getting frustrated or confused. These were all skills his condition and the medication took away from him.

The carers may not have been uncaring but they didn't give him the care his condition required. He needed someone to actually care for him.

I can't help but feel if the medical profession and those licensing the medication know what these side effects are, then a dietary list, monitoring and at least a healthy meal-delivery system should also be part of the treatment as people with schizophrenia no longer have the decision-making skills to look after themselves or the confidence to ask for help and advice, particularly when they're on the medication.

Of the total population that make up the 6% with type 2 diabetes, the mantra 'move more, eat less' is probably right. However, if they're on medication for mental disease of any kind, then the cause is most likely the medication's side effects and only a lifestyle change at the point of them first being prescribed it, can prevent it.

But even though Stewart ate less and, when his condition permitted, got out and moved about more than most people without diabetes, he still had little hope, because the medication was doing him harm and without the appropriate encouragement to make the right lifestyle changes before the diabetes struck, by the time he was diagnosed with diabetes, it was already probably too late.

So it seems until there is a will to find a better treatment for people with schizophrenia that isn't purely drug based and until healthcare moves away from being the slave of pharmaceuticals and focuses on the individual, there is nothing we can do to save people like my best friend Stewart.

The moment that cruel disease struck him down and he was put on an antipsychotic drug treatment, he was playing an unwitting game of Russian roulette, the end result being his death.

At least understanding this now brings a joy to my heart, knowing that both before those dark days of the evil empire and in those years of discovery, adventure and fun that followed on after, he at least enjoyed a fun and fulfilling life for the short time he had left and that, unlike a lot of us who will spend weeks in bed waiting to die, his end was mercifully short and from the moment he was unconscious his troubled mind would have seen him off in peace.

40

He may have no headstone but if a person continues to exist because their name is written down, then this ensures he'll exist eternally.

- Stewart Leonard Allen
- 11 July 1967 - 14 August 2017
- The Rose Garden Plot B2 Margate Cemetery.

Farewell my friend. Life is forever poorer without you by my side, without your cheeky humour and gentle innocence to approaching anything new. The cycle ride to the shops will always seem to meander more slowly now and as the shadows grow long and my senses dull, and time starts to slip away, you will always be that treasure that will make me smile and be thankful I once walked in the sun.

THE END

ABOUT THE AUTHOR

Anthony Day was born in Margate, Kent and now lives in Whitstable writing contemporary, science fiction, fantasy and historically based fiction.

OTHER BOOKS BY THIS AUTHOR INCLUDE

MUNCH
THE SIGNAL
THE CŒUR D'OR MYSTERY
WAITING FOR A TRAIN
CALICO JACK OF THE BLACK FLAG: vol 1
CALICO JACK OF THE BLACK FLAG: vol 2

Printed in Great Britain
by Amazon

33506683R00119